50¢

FALCONGUIDE®

BEST EASY DAY HIKES SERIES

best
easy
day hikes
Death Valley

Bill Cunningham
Polly Burke

D0180590

FALCONGUIDE®

GUILFORD, CONNECTICUT
HELENA, MONTANA

AN IMPRINT OF THE GLOBE PEQUOT PRESS

A FALCON GUIDE®

© 2004 Morris Book Publishing, LLC
Previously published by Falcon Publishing, Inc.

Falcon and FalconGuide are registered trademarks of Morris
Book Publishing, LLC.

Library of Congress Cataloging-in-Publication Data is
available.

ISBN-13: 978-1-56044-977-5
ISBN-10: 1-56044-977-2

Printed in Canada
First Edition/Fourth Printing

To buy books in quantity for corporate use
or incentives, call **(800) 962-0973, ext. 4551,**
or e-mail **premiums@GlobePequot.com.**

Contents

Map Legend

Interstate Highway/Freeway	(00)	City	# or ○	
US Highway	(00)	Campground	▲	
State or Other Principal Road	(00) (000)	Picnic Area	⌐	
Forest Road	(00)	Building	■	
Interstate Highway	⟹	Peak	⛰ 9,782 ft.	
Paved Road	⟹	Elevation	9,782 ft. ✕	
Gravel Road	⟹	River/Creek	～	
Unimproved Road	=====⟹	Spring	○⟋	
Trailhead	○	Pass	)(	
Parking Area	Ⓟ	Mine Site	⚒	
Main Trail/Route	▬▬▬	Sand Dunes	▬▬	
Main Trail/Route on Road	▬▬▬	Overlook	▫	
Alternate/Secondary Trail/Route	---⌃---	Forest/Park Boundary	⌐ ⌐	
Alternate/Secondary Trail/Route on Road	▬▬▬	State/International Border	▬ ▬ ▬	
One Way Road	One Way	Map Orientation	N ▲	
Road Junction	□	Scale	0 0.5 1 Miles	

v

Overview Map of
Death Valley National Park

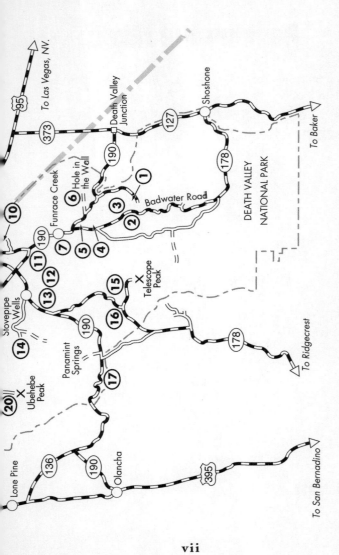

Ranking the Hikes

The following list ranks the hikes in this book from easiest to hardest. The ranking applies only to the primary hike described, not to any options that may be included.

Introduction

Death Valley National Park contains some of the planet's most imposing and contrasting landscapes—from North America's hottest, driest, and lowest desert to soaring snowcapped peaks. With such extremes, Death Valley commands respect and entices discovery.

The California Desert Protection Act of 1994 upgraded and expanded the 2-million-acre Death Valley National Monument into today's 3.3-million-acre national park, 95 percent of which is designated and managed as wilderness under the landmark 1964 Wilderness Act.

Despite its ominous name, Death Valley is home to more than 400 wildlife species, three-quarters of which are birds. Most wildlife is nocturnal and usually unseen by the human eye. Your day hikes in the park will reveal spectacular desert scenery, complex geology, primeval wilderness, historical and cultural sites, and perhaps even a fleeting glimpse of rare wildlife.

Best Easy Day Hikes Death Valley is a shortened and updated version of the Death Valley National Park section of *Hiking California's Desert Parks*. This compact guidebook features easily accessible hikes that appeal to the full spectrum of visitors—from kids to grandparents. These 23 hikes sample the best that Death Valley has to offer, for the casual hiker and also for those in search of a mellow start to a longer, more difficult hike.

Most of the hikes in *Best Easy Day Hikes Death Valley* are short—less than 4 miles round-trip and with less than 600 feet of elevation change. More than half the hikes are ideal for families with small children. All of the trailheads can be reached with a passenger car, and about one-third are accessed by a paved road. The best easy day hikes are well distributed throughout the more accessible central portion of the sprawling park, which is served by paved highways going north-to-south and east-to-west.

For the most part, options listed at the end of each hike description are extensions or longer variations of the hike. Consider these if you find yourself with that wonderful combination of additional time, energy, and determination.

Please keep in mind the park has very few developed trails. Wildrose Peak and Telescope Peak are the only backcountry trails maintained by the park. Most hiking is up canyons, across salt flats and alluvial fans, or over dunes where any trail would soon be erased by ever-shifting sands. Fortunately, hiking on these natural trails is often easier than on constructed paths.

To provide a geographic reference, Hikes 1 through 7 are located south of Furnace Creek in the southeastern region of the park. Hikes 8 through 23 are in the northwest section of the park, both west and north of Furnace Creek.

The hikes presented in this book are rated according to difficulty, from easier to hardest. The "Ranking the Hikes" page will help you choose suitable hikes for everyone in your party.

—*Bill Cunningham & Polly Burke*

How To Use This Guide

Types of Hikes

Loop: A loop hike begins and ends at the same trailhead without duplication of all or most of the route. If there is any retracing of the route it is only for a short distance. Round-trip mileage is provided for loop hikes.

Out-and-back: Out-and-back hikes reach a specific destination and return via the same route. Round-trip mileage is provided for out-and-back hikes.

Shuttle: A shuttle hike is a point-to-point route requiring a car shuttle between the starting and ending trailheads. The mileage is the total distance between the two trailheads.

Use Trail: A use trail is an obvious footpath that is not maintained by the park or another agency.

How To Get There

Primary access to the park from the south is via California 127 from Interstate 15 at Baker. CA 178 leads west into the park from CA 127 near Shoshone. CA 190 heads west into the park from CA 127 at Death Valley Junction. On the west side, CA 178 takes off from U.S. Highway 395 and enters the park by way of Panamint Valley. CA 190 takes off to the east from US 395 at Olancha, entering the park just west of Panamint Springs.

Weather

Recorded temperatures range from a sizzling 134 degrees to a freezing low of 15 degrees. An annual average of less than 2 inches of rain falls in the valley. Summer temperatures average well above 100 degrees. In general, temperatures will be 3 to 5 degrees cooler, along with increased precipitation for every 1,000-foot vertical increase in elevation. For hiking comfort, the months of November to April are hard to beat. Average highs are in the 60- to 90-degree range on the valley floor, cooling considerably at higher elevations. The higher peaks and ridges are often snow-covered from November to May.

Maps and Other Information

The map referred to as Trails Illustrated Death Valley National Park Map in the map section for each hike is the Death Valley National Park topographic backcountry and hiking map (1:160,000 scale), published by Trails Illustrated/National Geographic.

In general, the more detailed 7.5-minute USGS quadrangle maps (1:24,000 scale) listed for each hike are not needed for hikes of less than 2 miles unless you are venturing beyond the described route. Refer to the small-scale maps provided in this book, especially for shorter interpretative trails that are typically well signed.

The park entrance fee of $10 per vehicle or $5 if you're on foot or bicycle is valid for seven days. Golden Eagle and Golden Access passes are honored as well.

For current information on park regulations, weather,

campgrounds, park resources, hiking trails, and road conditions, contact Death Valley National Park, P.O. Box 579, Death Valley, CA 92328-0579; (760) 786-2331.

The Furnace Creek Visitor Center is open daily from 8 A.M. to 6 P.M. Ranger-guided hikes are offered during the peak season of November through April. Before you begin hiking, be sure to stop at the visitor center or a ranger station to get updated regulations and other information that will make your trip more enjoyable.

The website for the park is www.nps.gov/deva/. You can check the official park website for weekly ranger programs, including ranger-guided walks offered during the peak season of November through April. You can also use the website to request a park map and brochure by sending an e-mail to the National Park Service Office of Public Affairs.

Death Valley is busiest from February through mid-April, and in November. Surprisingly, the lowest visitation occurs during December and January, not during the hot summer months as you might expect.

Wildflowers

Rain throughout winter and spring, along with warm, sunny days and lack of drying winds, produce good wildflower years.

The park hosts more than 1,000 plant species, including 13 species of cactus and 23 species endemic to the region. Desert annuals, like poppies and primroses, are the showiest.

Typical peak blooming periods are:
- Mid-February to mid-April at lower elevations (the valley floor and alluvial fans).
- Early April to early May for elevations between 2,000 feet to 4,000 feet.
- Late April to early June for elevations above 4,000 feet.

Photography

The land of extremes that is Death Valley is best dramatized for the photographer when 11,049-foot Telescope Peak casts its afternoon shadow across the 282-feet-below-sea-level Badwater Basin. Combine this astounding vertical relief with recent volcanic craters, towering sand dunes, and flood-scoured canyons, and you'll see why knowledgeable photographers bring lots of extra film. These geologic wonders are most spectacular during the low-angle-light hours of morning and evening. Sunrises and sunsets are awe-inspiring.

Campgrounds

To reserve a campsite in one of the campgrounds in the park, call 1-800-436-PARK (7275). Camping fees range from $10 to $16 per night.

Play It Safe

Wandering in the desert has a reputation of being a dangerous activity, thanks to both the Bible and Hollywood. Usually depicted as a wasteland, the desert evokes fear. With proper planning, however, desert hiking can be fun, exciting, and quite safe.

An enjoyable desert outing requires preparation. Beginning with this book, you need to be equipped with adequate knowledge about your hiking area. The potential hazards of desert hiking can be mitigated if you are prepared.

Dehydration
Plenty of water is necessary for desert hiking. Carry one gallon per person per day in unbreakable plastic screw-top containers, and pause often to drink it. Always carry water, even on short, easy hikes. Keep a gallon of water in your car so you have some available at the end of your outing, too.

Changeable Weather
The desert is well known for sudden changes in the weather. The temperature can change 50 degrees in less than an hour. Prepare yourself with extra food and clothing, rain and wind gear, and a flashlight.

Hypothermia/Hyperthermia
Abrupt chilling is as much a danger in the desert as heat stroke. Storms and/or nightfall can cause desert tempera-

tures to plunge. Wear layers of clothes, adding or subtracting depending on conditions, to avoid overheating or chilling. At the other extreme, you need to protect yourself from sun and wind with proper clothing. The broad-brimmed hat is mandatory equipment for the desert traveler. Even in the cool days of winter, a delightful time in the desert, the sun's rays are intense. Don't forget the sunscreen.

Flash Floods

Desert washes and canyons can trap unwary visitors when rainstorms hit the desert. Keep a watchful eye on the sky. Check at a ranger station for regional weather conditions before embarking on your backcountry expedition. A storm anywhere upstream in the drainage can cause a sudden torrent in a lower canyon. Do not cross a flooded wash. Both the depth and the current can be deceiving. Wait for the flood to recede, which usually does not take long, before crossing.

Lightning

Be aware of lightning, especially during summer storms. Stay off ridges and peaks during storms. Shallow overhangs and gullies should also be avoided because electrical current often moves at ground level near a lightning strike.

Rattlesnakes, Scorpions, and Tarantulas

These desert "creepy crawlies" are easily terrified by unexpected human visitors, and they react predictably to being frightened. Do not sit or put your hands in dark places, especially during the warmer "snake-season" months.

Mine Hazards
Death Valley National Park contains numerous deserted mines. All of them should be considered hazardous. Stay away from all mines and mine structures. Many of these mines have not been secured or posted. Keep an eye on young or adventuresome members of your group.

Hantavirus
Hantavirus is a deadly disease carried by deer mice in the Southwest. Any enclosed area increases the chances of breathing the airborne particles that carry this life-threatening virus. There are often deserted buildings around Death Valley mine sites. As a precaution, do not enter deserted buildings.

Unstable Rocky Slopes
Desert canyons and mountainsides often consist of crumbly or fragmented rock. Use caution when climbing; however, the downward journey is usually the more hazardous. Smooth rock faces such as those found in slickrock canyons are equally dangerous, especially when you've got sand on the soles of your boots. On those rare occasions when they are wet, these rocks are slicker than ice.

Zero Impact

The desert environment is fragile; damage lasts for decades—even centuries. Desert courtesy requires us to leave no evidence that we were ever there. This ethic means no graffiti or defoliation at one end of the spectrum, and no unnecessary footprints on delicate vegetation on the other. Desert vegetation grows very slowly. Its destruction leads to wind and water erosion and irreparable harm to the desert.

The Falcon Zero-Impact Principles

- *Leave with everything you brought with you.*
- *Leave no sign of your visit.*
- *Leave the landscape as you found it.*

Avoid making new trails. If hiking cross-country, groups should follow one set of footprints. Try to make your route invisible. Darker crusty soil that crumbles easily indicates cryptogamic soils, which are a living blend of tightly bonded mosses, lichens, and bacteria. This dark crust prevents wind and water erosion and protects seeds that fall into the soil. Take special care to avoid stepping on this fragile layer.

Keep noise down. Desert wilderness means quiet and solitude, for animals and human visitors.

Leave your pets at home. Death Valley National Park forbids dogs on trails. It is never a good season for leaving your pet in your automobile, so share other experiences with your best friend, not Death Valley.

Pack it in and pack it out. This ethic is truer in the desert than anywhere else. Desert winds spread debris, and desert air preserves it. Always carry a trash bag, both for your trash and for any that you encounter. If you must smoke, pick up your butts and bag them.

Remember, artifacts fifty years old or older are protected by federal law and must not be disturbed.

Treat human waste properly. Bury waste four inches deep and at least 200 feet from water sources and trails. Pack out toilet paper and feminine hygiene products; they do not decompose in the arid desert. Do not burn toilet paper; many wildfires have been started this way.

Respect wildlife. Living in the desert is hard enough for the wildlife without being harassed by human intruders. Be respectful and use binoculars for long-distance viewing. Do not molest the rare desert water sources by playing or bathing in them.

Enjoy the beauty and solitude of the desert, and leave it for others to enjoy.

Hiker's Checklist

Use the following checklist as you assemble your gear for day hiking in the California desert.

Day Hike

- sturdy, well-broken-in, light-to-medium weight hiking boots
- broad-brimmed hat, which must be wind-proof
- long-sleeved shirt for sun protection
- long pants for protection against sun and brush
- water; 2 quarts to 1 gallon/day (depending on season), in sturdy screw-top plastic containers
- large-scale topo map and compass (adjusted for magnetic declination)
- whistle, mirror, and matches (for emergency signals)
- flashlight (in case your hike takes longer than you expect)
- sunblock and lip sunscreen
- insect repellent (in season)
- pocketknife
- small first-aid kit: tweezers, bandages, antiseptic, moleskin, snakebite extractor kit
- bee sting kit (over the counter antihistamine or epinephrine by prescription) as needed for the season
- windbreaker (or rain gear in season)
- lunch or snack, with plastic bag for your trash
- toilet paper, with a plastic zipper bag to pack it out
- your FalconGuide

Optional Gear

- camera and film
- binoculars
- bird and plant guidebooks
- notebook and pen/pencil

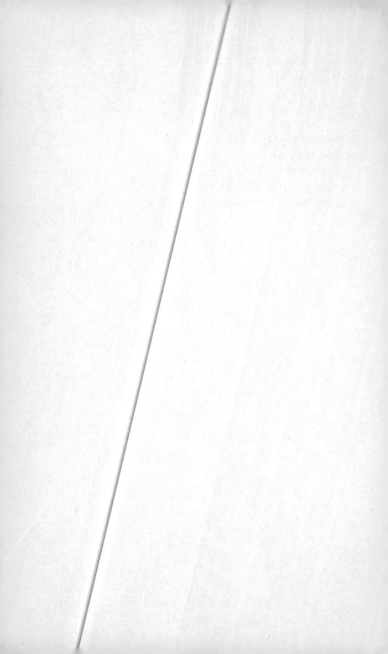

1
DANTES VIEW AND POINT

Highlights: Dantes View offers some of the most magnificent panoramic views found anywhere, overlooking the astounding vertical relief between the highest point in Death Valley National Park and lowest point in the continental United States.
Type of hike: Out-and-back.
Total distance: 1 mile.
Elevation gain: 229 feet.
Best months: October–June.
Maps: Trails Illustrated Death Valley National Park Map; USGS Dantes View quad.
Parking and trailhead facilities: There is a large signed parking area at the end of the paved road.

Finding the trailhead: From California 190, 11.9 miles southeast of the Furnace Creek Visitor Center and 18 miles west of Death Valley Junction, turn south on the signed Dantes View Road (paved, all-weather). Drive 13.2 miles on this steep, winding road to its end at the Dantes View parking area. The unsigned trail to Dantes Point is clearly visible to the north as it climbs toward Dantes Point from the parking area.

Dantes View and Point

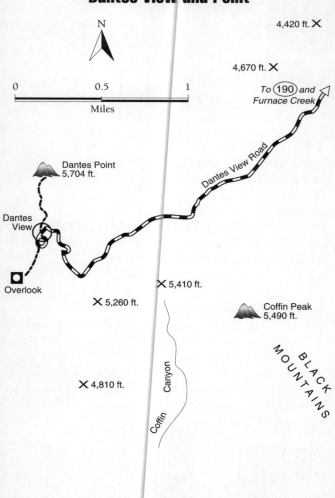

N

0   0.5   1
Miles

4,420 ft. ✕

4,670 ft. ✕

To ⑲⓪ and
Furnace Creek

Dantes View Road

Dantes Point
5,704 ft.

Dantes
View

Overlook

✕ 5,410 ft.

✕ 5,260 ft.

Coffin Peak
5,490 ft.

✕ 4,810 ft.

Coffin Canyon

BLACK MOUNTAINS

Key points:
0.0 Trailhead.
0.3 The trail intersects the summit ridge.
0.5 Reach Dantes Point (5,704 feet).

The hike: If possible, take this hike in the early morning with the sun at your back. This makes for better photography and for enhanced enjoyment of the superlative vistas and astounding 5,755-foot drop to the salt flats of Badwater, which sits 282 feet below sea level. The temperature at Dantes View averages 25 degrees cooler than that of Badwater. This exposed location is usually windy, necessitating a windbreak garment for the hike.

This lofty vantage point in the Black Mountains enables you to almost see, or at least visualize, how the mountains are both rising and slowly moving to the left (south) relative to the surrounding terrain. Looking across Death Valley to the highest point in the park, 11,049-foot Telescope Peak, it is easy to note the major vegetative life zones stretching westward like a giant map. Bristlecone and limber pines thrive high in the Panamint Range. Below is the pinyon pine–juniper zone. Dantes View is situated in a hotter, drier midslope of blackbush and sage. Floods from the mountains result in graveled fans that support spreading root species such as creosote bush. Freshwater displaces salt from the fan edges, allowing mesquite to grow. Pickleweed gains a foothold in the brackish water below these edges. The muddy tans and grays of the valley floor grade into white beds of almost pure salt—a chemical desert.

From the parking lot, hike north along the road for 0.1 mile to where the Dantes Point trail begins a fairly steep climb up the hill. Soon it winds to the left (west) and contours gently along the mountain's west slope. This route provides an even more impressive view down to Badwater, with an almost overwhelming sense of vertical relief dropping more than a mile straight down! At 0.3 mile, the trail intersects the summit ridge, then climbs the short distance to the 5,704-foot-high point. Although unofficial, the trail is clear, well defined, and easy to follow. Return the way you came to complete this 1-mile out-and-back ridge walk, and don't forget the film.

Options: For a slightly different perspective, hike a well-used path 0.25 mile southwest of the parking area. The rock outcropping at the point of the ridge is especially useful as a windbreak for setting up a tripod for early morning photography.

After reaching Dantes Point, you can hike off-trail for another 3.5 miles to Mount Perry.

Another scenic, nearby option is the 2.4-mile off-trail hike to cone-shaped Coffin Peak (5,490 feet) on the south side of Dantes View Road. The parking pullout is about 0.5 mile before you reach the Dantes View parking area. The ridge to the peak wraps around its east side, where a faint use trail leads to the summit. Most of this ridge route is within view of Dantes View Road. This vantage point in the Black Mountains offers breathtaking vistas without the crowds of Dantes View.

2
BADWATER

Highlights: A vast bed of salt in the hottest, lowest spot in the United States, 280 feet below sea level.

Type of hike: Out-and-back.

Total distance: 1 to 2 miles.

Elevation gain: Minimal.

Best months: Late October–March.

Maps: Trails Illustrated Death Valley National Park Map; USGS Badwater quad.

Parking and trailhead facilities: There is a signed parking area alongside a paved highway.

Finding the trailhead: The signed parking area for Badwater is on the west side of California 178 (Badwater Road), 16.7 miles south of the CA 190/178 junction at the Furnace Creek Inn.

Key points:

0.0 Trailhead.

0.5 Reach the edge of the salt flats.

The hike: As bleak as it looks, the popular hike onto the salt flats at Badwater is arguably the ultimate Death Valley experience. If you have been to Dantes View or Telescope Peak, you probably saw the human ants on the white

Badwater

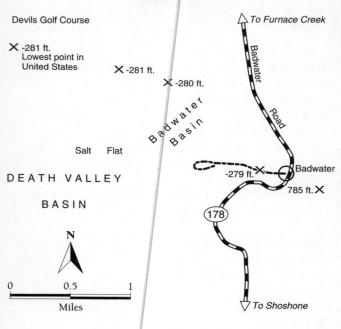

Devils Golf Course

✕ -281 ft.
Lowest point in
United States

✕ -281 ft.

✕ -280 ft.

Badwater Basin

Salt   Flat

DEATH VALLEY

BASIN

N

0   0.5   1

Miles

To Furnace Creek

Badwater   Road

-279 ft. ✕   ⊙ Badwater

785 ft. ✕

178

To Shoshone

expanse of valley floor and wondered what could be so fascinating. Here you will find individuals, especially families, cavorting like they're at the beach or enjoying a spring snow. To gain a genuine sense of the enormity of the salt flats, hike beyond the heavily traveled section.

The hike begins at the parking area beneath the cliffs that soar up to Dantes View, 5,755 feet above. There's a "Sea Level" sign on the cliff face, high above Badwater, making very clear what minus 280 feet represent. Walk out to the salt flats on the causeway, but continue beyond the well-trod area, depending on the temperature and wind, to a clear area of the flats. Getting away from the highway is essential to get a sense of the magnitude of the salt flats. You'll reach the edge of the 5-mile-wide salt flats after only 0.5 mile.

Here, fresh salt crystals are forming as groundwater percolates to the surface, bringing salt that crystallizes as the water hastily evaporates—chemistry in action. If you sit on the salt flats, you will find yourself among tiny salt pinnacles, a miniature mountainous world at the bottom of this mountainous basin. In close contact with the surface you will also discover that salt is a tough commodity. The white flooring of the flats is only inches thick, but very firm underfoot. Salt's power as an erosive force is noteworthy in this desert, where it functions much like frost heaves and ice do in a wet climate. Salt crystals grow and force apart boulders, breaking them down to be further eroded by wind and water. The salt crystal crust may be covered with a temporary lake following a rare heavy rain storm.

Above the microworld of salt, the world of Death Valley soars. To the west is Telescope Peak (11,048 feet), the highest point in the park, less than 20 miles away. The difference in elevation between Badwater and Telescope Peak is one of the largest in the United States.

A hike at Badwater is an essential introduction to the expanse of the valley floor. The emigrants and the miners who lived in this environment were a tough lot.

The glare from the salt flats can be as intense as on snow fields at high elevation. Wear sunglasses. Do not hike to the salt flats during the extreme heat of summer.

3
NATURAL BRIDGE

Highlights: Geological phenomena such as faults, slip fault-ing, chutes, dryfalls, and natural arch formation.
Type of hike: Out-and-back.
Total distance: 2 miles.
Elevation gain: 520 feet.
Best months: October–April.
Maps: Trails Illustrated Death Valley National Park Map; USGS Devils Golf Course quad.
Parking and trailhead facilities: There is a large signed park-ing area and an information kiosk at the end of the dirt road.

Finding the trailhead: From the intersection of California 190 and 178 in Furnace Creek, drive south on the Badwater Road (CA 178) for 14.1 miles. Turn left (east) on the signed dirt road, and drive 1.5 miles to the Natu-ral Bridge parking area. The road is washboardy and rough, but is suitable for standard two-wheel-drive ve-hicles. The trail begins behind the information kiosk.

Key points:
0.0 The trail heads northwest from parking area.
0.3 The natural bridge arcs over the trail.
0.8 Reach a small dryfall.
1.0 The canyon is blocked by a 20-foot dryfall.

Natural Bridge

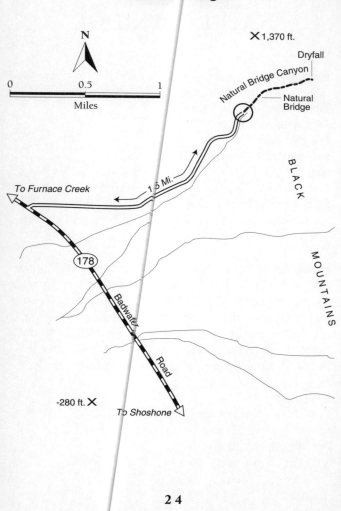

N

X 1,370 ft.

Dryfall

Natural Bridge Canyon

Natural Bridge

0   0.5   1
Miles

BLACK

To Furnace Creek

1.5 Mi.

M
O
U
N
T
A
I
N
S

178

Badwater

Road

-280 ft. X

To Shoshone

The hike: Death Valley's fascinating geologic history is featured on the informational kiosk at the trailhead of the Natural Bridge hike. Bedding and slip faulting are explained on the board, so the canyon's convoluted display is even more impressive. Likewise, differential erosion is described and illustrated, preparing you for the bridge. Fault caves, the metamorphic layers of the Artists Drive Formation, and mud drips are other topics covered in this condensed, well written version of physical geology. The kiosk is worth visiting before embarking on this hike.

The canyon floor consists of loose gravel; that and its sharp slope suggest a relatively young canyon. Death Valley's floor continues to subside while the Funeral Mountains rise. Dynamic geologic forces are still active here.

The trail begins by passing through deeply eroded volcanic ash and pumice canyon walls. The gravel wash maintains a steady 6 percent grade as the canyon gradually narrows. At 0.3 mile, the high bridge arches over the canyon bottom. An ancient streambed is visible to the north of the bridge, where floods swept around this more resistant section of stratum before the pothole beneath it gave way to form the natural bridge.

Beyond the bridge, mud drips, slip faults, and fault caves appear, reinforcing the information you picked up at the kiosk. You can climb a dryfall at mile 0.8 with moderate effort, but a 20-foot dryfall blocks travel at 1 mile.

Retracing your steps down the canyon reveals even more examples of geology in action. Ever-shifting light creates iridescent colors. Traveling in the same direction as the powerful flash floods and the loads of scouring debris emphasizes the impact of water in this arid environment.

4
DESOLATION NARROWS

Highlights: This deep, narrow, colorful canyon provides a feeling of solitude, with broad vistas at the overlook.
Type of hike: Out-and-back.
Total distance: 1 mile to narrows; 3.2 miles to overlook.
Elevation gain: Minimal to canyon narrows; 680 feet to overlook.
Best months: Early November–mid-April.
Maps: Trails Illustrated Death Valley National Park Map; USGS Furnace Creek quad.
Parking and trailhead facilities: You can park alongside the dirt road at its end.

Finding the trailhead: From the park visitor center at Furnace Creek, drive south 1 mile to the junction of California 190 and 178 (at the Furnace Creek Inn). Turn right (south) onto CA 178 (Badwater Road), and drive 3.9 miles to the unsigned dirt road that takes off to the left (east) from the highway. Drive 1 mile to the end of this relatively smooth dirt road and park. Desolation Canyon is to the immediate left (northeast) of the road. Follow one of several well-worn paths that lead northeast over the low ridge to the broad lower end of Desolation Canyon.

Desolation Narrows

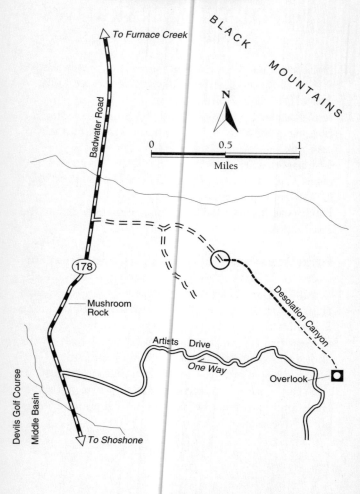

To Furnace Creek

BLACK MOUNTAINS

Badwater Road

N

0   0.5   1
Miles

178

Mushroom
Rock

Desolation Canyon

Artists   Drive
One Way

Overlook

Devils Golf Course

Middle Basin

To Shoshone

Key points:

0.0 Trailhead and parking area.
0.1 Reach the intersection with the Desolation Canyon wash; turn right up the canyon.
0.3 The canyon splits; stay right.
0.4 At the canyon junction stay right up the main wash.
0.5 The canyon narrows.

Optional hike to overlook:

0.7 The canyon widens to a junction; go right up the steeper, less-colorful canyon with more stair-step rocks.
1.1 At the canyon junction stay right up a narrow gully.
1.5 The canyon reaches a steep chute.
1.6 Scramble up a very steep, unstable slope on the right to the overlook.

The hike: This hike is a highly scenic but less crowded alternative to the nearby Golden Canyon hike (Hike 5). The optional extended hike involves moderate canyoneering to a high pass overlooking the Artists Drive Formation. Despite its proximity to both the Badwater Road and Artists Drive, the narrow canyon provides a deep feeling of intimacy and solitude. The entire out-and-back trip provides a superb opportunity to observe the dynamics of badlands erosion, from mud-filled gullies to bizarre eroded shapes overlooking the canyon.

Because Desolation Canyon involves a short hike at low elevation, the recommended time of day for the hike is mid- to late afternoon, when the cooler shadows fill the canyon. Upon return, in late afternoon to early evening, the brilliant light can be spectacular on the multicolored east-facing slopes above the canyon.

The main Desolation Canyon is just over the low ridge to the north from the end-of-the-road trailhead. Upon reaching the canyon in 0.1 mile, turn right (southeast) and head up the wide wash that climbs gently to the first canyon junction at 0.3 mile; stay to the right. Continue right at the next junction at 0.4 mile. At 0.5 mile, the canyon narrows with even narrower side draws. In places, the canyon is narrow enough that you can touch both sides at once. Retrace your route to complete this 1-mile round trip to the canyon narrows.

Option: The hike can be extended to the head of the canyon or slightly beyond to an overlook. The next 0.1 mile brings a couple of stair-step rocks that are easy to climb, before the canyon again widens. At 1.1 miles, what appears to be the main canyon to the left ends at a dry waterfall another 0.1 mile up. Continue up the narrowing canyon to the right; it ends at a steep, unstable rock chute at 1.5 miles. This is a good turnaround point.

If you've still got the urge and energy to explore, climb up to the right on loose, deep gravel to the overlook at 1.6 miles, which is at 740 feet in elevation. This relatively lofty vantage point provides a spectacular view of the varied colors of the Artists Drive Formation to the south. From this point, the Artists Drive is only about 0.3 mile west. Return by way of Desolation Canyon to complete this colorful 3.2-mile round-trip badlands/canyon excursion.

5
GOLDEN CANYON
INTERPRETIVE TRAIL

Highlights: An educational geology trail, colorful lakebed, exposed strata, alluvial fan formations; spectacular scenery.

Type of hike: Out-and-back.

Total distance: 2 miles (6.5 miles for complete optional loop with side trips).

Elevation gain: 300 feet (950 feet for the complete loop).

Best months: November–April.

Maps: Trails Illustrated Death Valley National Park Map; USGS Furnace Creek quad.

Parking and trailhead facilities: The signed trailhead and parking area, with information kiosk, is adjacent to the paved highway.

Finding the trailhead: From California 190, 1.2 miles south of the Furnace Creek Visitor Center, head south on the paved Badwater Road (CA 178). After 2 miles, turn left (east) into the Golden Canyon parking area and trailhead, which is on the east side of the road. From the south, 2 miles north of the small town of Shoshone, turn west onto CA 178 and continue into the park. From Ashford Junction, go north on Badwater Road. The signed Golden Canyon parking area is 14.4 miles north of Badwater and can be seen just off the highway to the right (east).

Golden Canyon Interpretive Trail

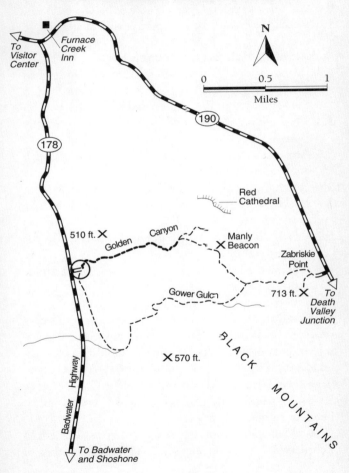

To Visitor Center

Furnace Creek Inn

190

178

N

0   0.5   1
Miles

Red Cathedral

510 ft. ✕   Golden   Canyon

Manly Beacon ✕

Zabriskie Point

Gower Gulch

713 ft. ✕

To Death Valley Junction

✕ 570 ft.

BLACK MOUNTAINS

Badwater Highway

To Badwater and Shoshone

Key points:
0.0 Golden Canyon trailhead (160 feet below sea level).
1.0 Reach the end of the interpretive trail at stop 10.

Optional intermediate points or complete loop:
1.8 Reach the intersection with the 0.8-mile side trip to
     the base of Red Cathedral. Backtrack to stop 10 and
     the beginning of the trail toward Manly Beacon.
2.3 The high point of the trail (440 feet) is below Manly
     Beacon.
2.6 Arrive at a trail/wash junction between Gower Gulch
     and Zabriskie Point
3.6 Reach the overlook below Zabriskie Point (500 feet).
3.8 Backtrack to the trail/wash junction; begin to hike
     down Gower Gulch.
5.2 Reach the 30-foot dryfall in Gower Gulch; take the
     trail around to the right.
6.5 Complete the loop back at the Golden Canyon trail-
     head.

The hike: Both the shorter and longer versions of this hike
provide a fascinating journey through geologic time, passing rocks of different ages as the elevation increases. An
excellent interpretive trail guide to the Golden Canyon
Trail is available for 50 cents at the Golden Canyon Trailhead. Ten stops in this geology guide are keyed to num-
bered posts along the trail.

Golden Canyon was once accessed by paved road. In
February 1976, a four-day storm caused 2.3 inches of

rain to fall on nearby Furnace Creek—one of the driest places on earth (where no rain fell during all of 1929 and 1953). Runoff from the torrential cloudburst undermined and washed out the pavement, so that today Golden Canyon is a wonderful place for hikers only. This pattern of drought and torrent follows countless periods of flash floods, shattering rockslides, and a wetter era when the alluvial fan was preceded by an ancient shallow sea. This is a land in constant flux.

At stop 2, it is easy to see how the canyon was carved out of an old alluvial fan made up of volcanic rock that predates Death Valley's origin some 3 million years ago. Layers in the rock tell the tales of periodic floods over the eons. Just above, the canyon displays tilted bands of rock, where faulting caused huge blocks of the earth's crust to slide past one another. The Furnace Creek formation is the compilation over time of lakebed sediments dating back about 9 million years. The ripple marks of water lapping over the sandy lakebed hardened into stone as the climate warmed; the marks are evident on the tilted rock. Weathering and the effects of thermal water produced the splash of vivid colors seen today.

Mountain building to the west gradually produced a more arid climate, causing the lake to dry up. At the same time, the land was tilted by the widening and sinking of Death Valley and by the uplift of the Black Mountains. Dark lava from eruptions 3 to 5 million years ago slowed erosion, explaining why Manly Beacon juts so far above the surrounding badlands. These stark badlands rising above the canyon at mile 0.5 are the result of rapid run-off from storms on erodible, almost impermeable rocks.

Several narrow side canyons invite exploration on the way up Golden Canyon, particularly those opposite stop 2, and to the left and just above stops 6 and 7. The interpretive trail ends at stop 10, about 1 mile up the canyon at an elevation of 140 feet. For the short hike, this is your turnaround point.

Options: For a 0.8-mile round-trip hike to the base of the Red Cathedral, continue up the broken pavement. Hike past the old parking area to a narrow notch at 320 feet, directly below the cathedral's looming presence. Red Cathedral was once part of an active alluvial fan, outwashed from the Black Mountains to the south. The bright red color results from the weathering of iron to produce the rust of iron oxide. The cliff faces are made up of the more resistant red rock crowning softer yellow lake deposits.

Upon returning to stop 10 at mile 1.8, follow the signed trail to your left (east) up a steep gully well marked with trail posts. The trail climbs across badlands beneath the imposing sandstone jaw of Manly Beacon. At 2.3 miles, you reach a high ridge saddle below Manly Beacon at 440 feet. Follow the markers down a side gully to a wash/trail junction at 2.6 miles. The left-hand wash leads eastward up to Zabriskie Point. The right-hand wash/trail descends west to Gower Gulch.

If you walk up the main wash, you quickly come to the artificial cut made in the rock wall to divert Furnace

Creek through Gower Gulch. This cut has sped up erosion in the gulch. Note the gray color of the rocks washed in from Furnace Creek, which lie on the bottom of the drainage in contrast to the reds and yellows of the badlands. Gower Gulch is largely the result of human construction to protect Furnace Creek from serious flooding.

For a short side trip toward Zabriskie Point, turn left (south) at the junction and follow the markers for about 0.5 mile to excellent views of Zabriskie Point, the surrounding badlands, Death Valley, and the distant Panamint Range. Zabriskie Point is another 0.7 mile and 200 feet above, and is accessible by road from the other side. It does indeed provide one of the most magnificent views in all of Death Valley, but its proximity to a paved road may detract from the hiking experience on the Golden-Gower loop. Thus, the overlook below Zabriskie Point is recommended as the turnaround point for a scenic side trip. Zabriskie Point is a popular starting point for those hiking 3 miles downhill through Gower Gulch, then across to the mouth of Golden Canyon.

Back at the trail junction at mile 3.6, there is no marker post to point the way toward Gower Gulch. Simply continue down the wash toward wide, gray Gower Gulch, which drops below mounds of golden badlands. At 3.9 miles, a side wash intersects the main wash; continue downward to the right. Early-day miners in search of borax have pocketed the walls of Gower Gulch with tunnels. These small openings are unsecured and potentially dangerous. A mile down, the wide gravel wash bends sharply left, narrowing dramatically with the bedding and faulting of red and green rock. The canyon floor then quickly drops 40 feet to below sea level.

At 5.2 miles, the wash meets a 30-foot dryfall. A good use trail curves around the rock face to the right. From here, the faint but easy-to-follow trail heads north 1.3 miles along the base of the mountains, paralleling the highway back to the Golden Canyon parking area, completing the loop and side trips.

6
HOLE IN THE WALL NORTH

Highlights: The pitted surface of volcanic ash cliffs; dryfall; bighorn sheep habitat.
Type of hike: Loop.
Total distance: 2.8 miles.
Elevation gain: 540 feet.
Best months: October–March.
Maps: Trails Illustrated Death Valley National Park Map; USGS Furnace Creek and Echo Canyon quads.
Parking and trailhead facilities: Park alongside a rocky dirt road. There are no facilities.

Finding the trailhead: From the junction of California 190 and 178 in Furnace Creek, go southeast on CA 190 for 5.4 miles to the dirt road to Hole in the Wall , which is on the left. The road is in the wash; a sign recommending four-wheel-drive vehicles stands 40 feet west of the road itself, on the bank of the wash. The first 4 miles of the road are rough and rocky, but are passable by a passenger vehicle if you drive carefully. Drive 4 miles to the Hole in the Wall narrows and park. The hiking route heads directly north from the narrows. You'll need four-wheel drive beyond Hole in the Wall.

Hole In The Wall North

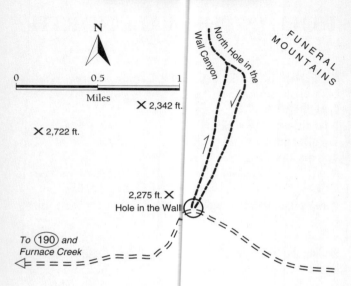

Key points:
0.0 Head north from notch where road turns east.
1.0 Reach the canyon mouth.
1.3 The canyon narrows; a dryfall blocks the canyon.
1.6 Head back down to the canyon mouth.
1.8 Hike east along the mountainside to the next canyon, blocked by boulders.
2.8 Hike south on the fan/wash back to the Hole in the
Wall Trailhead.

The hike: Located less than 10 miles from busy Furnace Creek, this excursion to a lower canyon entrance provides desert panoramas, solitude, majestic rock formations, and varied terrain. A short side trip to the neighboring canyon demonstrates the powers of nature here in the Funeral Mountains.

The hike begins at the Hole in the Wall cliffs, which are made of differentially eroded volcanic ash. The multitude of holes form enchanting shapes; some are precise, while others droop. To the north, beyond the alluvial fan, rise the Funeral Mountains. Travel north-northwest using the varnished desert pavement where possible since the wash winds a bit and is loaded with boulders that make hiking difficult. You gain 420 feet in elevation by the time you reach the canyon mouth at 1.0 mile.

Here, more towering limestone cliffs display the eyes and mouths of erosion holes. The canyon floor is a wide gravel wash. The canyon narrows and turns at 1.3 miles, only to be blocked by a 40-foot dryfall. The tempting side hill to the west is too unstable and dangerous for climbing, so this is the terminal point of the canyon hike. Instead, enjoy the vistas of the valley on your return trip.

At the canyon mouth, hike east 0.2 mile to the next canyon. This one is totally blocked by massive boulders, cutting all travel to its secret hinterland.

The return to Hole in the Wall features magnificent views of the Artists Drive Formation at the northern end of the Black Mountains, with Death Valley stretching out beyond. On the horizon, Telescope Peak stands at 11,048 feet. This is a spectacular array of Death Valley scenery.

Harmony Borax Works

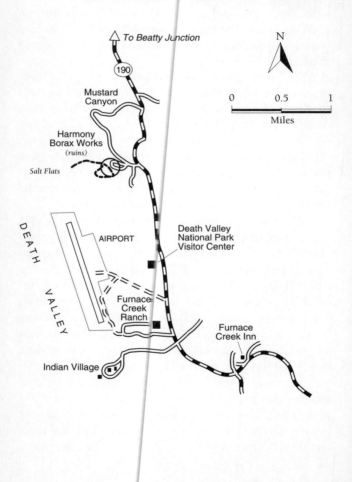

To Beatty Junction

190

Mustard
Canyon

Harmony
Borax Works
(ruins)

Salt Flats

N

0   0.5   1
Miles

D
E
A
T
H

V
A
L
L
E
Y

AIRPORT

Death Valley
National Park
Visitor Center

Furnace
Creek
Ranch

Furnace
Creek Inn

Indian Village

7
HARMONY BORAX WORKS

Highlights: A historic nineteenth-century industrial site and salt flats.

Type of hike: Loop.

Total distance: 1 mile.

Elevation gain: Minimal.

Best months: October–March

Maps: Trails Illustrated Death Valley National Park Map; USGS Furnace Creek West and Furnace Creek quads. The USGS quads that cover the route are not required for this hike; refer to the map in this book.

Parking and trailhead facilities: The signed trailhead is close to the paved highway.

Finding the trailhead: The trailhead for the Harmony Borax Works Trail is 1.3 miles north of the park visitor center at Furnace Creek on California 190. The 0.2-mile road on the left (west) is signed. The asphalt walkway leads west of the parking area. The optional 5-mile round-trip hike to the salt flats begins at the far side of Harmony Borax Works, heading west from the loop trail.

Key points:

0.0 Harmony Borax Works Trailhead.

0.2 A trail leads south from the asphalt path to the hilltop.

0.5 Reach the outer end of loop; the use trail extends out into the salt flats.

The hike: This desolate site was the scene of frenzied activity from 1883 to 1888—not in quest of gold, like so much mining activity, but of borax. Used in ceramics and glass as well as soap and detergent, borax was readily available here in Death Valley. Borax prices were mercurial due to soaring supply and moderate demand in the nineteenth century, so the industry was plagued by sharp boom and bust cycles. Here at the Harmony Works, the years of prosperity were typically brief.

Chinese laborers hauled the borate sludge in from the flats on sledges to the processing plant, the remains of which are the focal point of the hike. There, the borate was boiled down and hauled 165 miles across the desert to Mojave by the famed twenty-mule teams. One of the wagons that made this journey stands below the borax plant. Although the works were in operation only from October to June, working conditions for man and beast were harsh. The hike on the paved loop trail is short but dehydrating. Be sure to bring water.

Options: A 0.5-mile side hike to a low hilltop overlook gives you an excellent vista of the central valley floor. From here, it is easy to imagine the usual workday in operation at the Harmony Works. To the east of the hilltop is an area that appears to have been a dump for Furnace Creek. A rusty antique car rests on the hillside, surrounded by desert.

You can also reach Harmony Borax Works by way of a 1-mile-long bicycle path along CA 190 from Furnace Creek.

A longer optional hike to the salt flats —of about 5 miles round-trip—confirms the arduous nature of the work on the valley floor. An unsigned but well-trod path leads west from the end of the paved loop. It travels by a damp slough where groundwater percolates to the surface, causing borate crystals to form. Farther out on the flats, mounds of borax mud remain where the laborers made piles to validate the works' mining claim more than a hundred years ago.

Keane Spring
Monarch Canyon and Mine

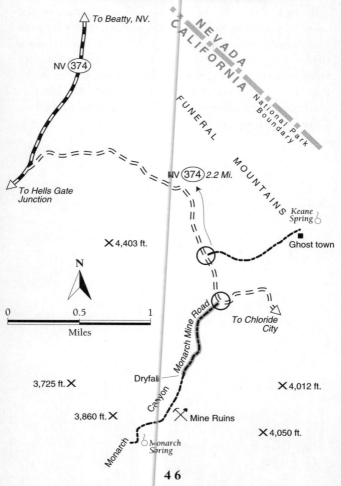

△ To Beatty, NV.

NV 374

NEVADA
CALIFORNIA

National Park Boundary

FUNERAL

⇙ To Hells Gate
Junction

NV 374 2.2 Mi.

MOUNTAINS

Keane
Spring ⚲

Ghost town ■

✕ 4,403 ft.

N

0   0.5   1
Miles

To Chloride
City ⇘

Monarch Mine Road

Dryfall

3,725 ft. ✕

3,860 ft. ✕

Monarch

Canyon

⚒ Mine Ruins

✕ 4,012 ft.

✕ 4,050 ft.

⚲ Monarch
Spring

8
KEANE SPRING

Highlights: An old town site and spring.
Type of hike: Out-and-back.
Total distance: 1 mile.
Elevation gain: 200 feet.
Best months: October–April.
Maps: Trails Illustrated Death Valley National Park Map; USGS Chloride City quad.
Parking and trailhead facilities: There is a parking area next to the barricaded dirt road at the trailhead.

Finding the trailhead: From Nevada 374 (Daylight Pass Road) 3.4 miles east of Hells Gate Junction in Boundary Canyon and 15.8 miles southwest of Beatty, Nevada, look for a road on the south side that is marked only with a small sign recommending four-wheel drive. Turn south, and drive 2 miles to a barricaded road taking off to the left (east) to the Keane ghost town and spring. This former road serves as the trail.

Key points:
0.0 Trailhead.
0.3 Continue northeast on the ridgetop.
0.4 Look for the remnants of the townsite.
0.5 Continue up the wash/trail to the spring.

The hike: The Keane Spring townsite attests to the value of desert water. The town's brief existence (1906–1909) was based entirely on the availability of water here. When the Funeral Mountains were humming with mining activity during the rhyolite gold boom, Keane Spring promoters counted on providing the water necessary for both miners and ore processing. Ironically, the town was wiped out in a 1909 flash flood.

Why was the town nestled in the wash below the spring? In these rolling foothills of the Funeral Mountains, the open country features panoramic views of Death Valley and Tucki Mountains but also guarantees intense wind. The wash presumably offered protection from the latter. Apparently town's opportunistic promoters ignored the dangers of flooding in the wash.

From the parking area, bear right and up on the faint trace of an old roadway toward a low ridge. At 0.3 mile, you will top out on the ridge. Continue northeast on an old road's path. Bright green willows mark the moisture of the spring in the depression ahead. Continue toward the greenery, heading downhill to the dry streambed. Follow the streambed to the dense foliage. The scattered remnants of the town of Keane Spring lie along the dry stream.

The only remains of the town are a few stone foundations left in tangled catclaw at 0.4 mile. Pieces of the old pipeline run from the spring to the southeast, in the direction of Chloride City, the primary water customer. Chloride City's brief period of prosperity was in 1906. The infamous San Francisco earthquake wiped out (economically) its investors, so Keane Spring was declining long before the flood arrived.

The spring's output has diminished since the beginning of this century. Now there is no visible flow—or even a gurgle of water—from the dense thicket of rushes and willows that jams the narrow spring, which is immediately above the Keane Spring town site at 0.5 mile. Birds and vegetation here demonstrate that enough moisture exists for nature to flourish. The coyote population is thriving also, judging from the droppings on the trail.

Keane Spring never was a very large town. With fewer than a dozen buildings and even fewer business establishments, its economic base was precariously thin. Nature has nearly erased its traces.

9
MONARCH CANYON
AND MINE

see map page 46

Highlights: Large, scenic dry waterfalls, bird watching, an historic stamp mill.
Type of hike: Out-and-back.
Total distance: 1.8 miles from the end of Monarch Mine Road; 3 miles from the Chloride City Road.
Elevation loss: 390 feet from the end of Monarch Mine Road; 570 feet from the Chloride City Road.
Best months: October–April.
Maps: Trails Illustrated Death Valley National Park Map; USGS Chloride City quad.
Parking and trailhead facilities: Park alongside an unsigned road junction, or at the end of the dirt road.

Finding the trailhead: From Nevada 374 (Daylight Pass Road) 3.4 miles east of Hells Gate Junction in Boundary Canyon and 15.8 miles southwest of Beatty, Nevada, look for a road to the south marked only with a small sign recommending four-wheel drive. Carefully driven high-clearance two-wheel-drive vehicles can negotiate this road for 2.2 miles to the bottom of upper Monarch Canyon. High-clearance four-wheel drive is required for vehicular travel beyond this point to Chloride City. The rough Monarch Mine Road takes off south from this point. This road junction can serve as the trailhead for the hike down Monarch Canyon. However, you can shorten the hike by 1.2 miles if you drive down the Monarch Mine Road to a point just above the dryfall; four-wheel drive is required.

Key points:
0.0 Trailhead at the junction of the Chloride City Road and Monarch Mine Road in upper Monarch Canyon.

0.6 Reach the end of Monarch Mine Road and an 80-foot dryfall.

0.7 The mining trail drops to the bottom of the canyon wash.

0.8 Walk up the wash to the base of the dry falls.

1.2 Reach the Monarch Mine stamp mill ruins.

1.5 Arrive at Monarch Spring.

The hike: You can start at the unsigned junction between the rough Chloride City Road and four-wheel-drive Monarch Mine Road (3 miles round-trip to Monarch Spring) or at the end of the Monarch Mine Road (1.8 miles round-trip). From the Chloride City Road junction, the trip starts out in rounded, low-lying hills. The four-wheel-drive road descends southwesterly, entering a rocky canyon after 0.3 mile.

At 0.6 mile, the road ends above a striking 80-foot dryfall. A major side canyon enters from the left, bounded by high cliffs marked by folded multicolored bands of rock. Continue left around the fall on the old mining trail. After another 0.1 mile, the trail drops to the wash, which is covered with horsetails and Mormon tea. This is favored habitat for quail and other birds. The base of the dryfall is definitely worth visiting, so turn right and walk 0.1 mile up to the precipice. In addition to the main wide falls, another smaller but equally high fall guards the canyon bowl to the left. The canyon walls are distinguished by shelf rock catch basins, overhangs, and contorted layers of colorful, twisted rock.

Proceeding down the sandy canyon wash, an eroded mining trail crosses to the right and then drops back to the canyon floor at 1 mile. Cairns are in place for the return trip. At 1.2 miles, you reach the wood and cement ruins of the Monarch Mine stamp mill on the left (southeast). The ore chute to the mill extends up an almost vertical rock face.

To further experience the rugged grandeur of Monarch Canyon, continue down the wash another 0.3 mile to the brushy bottom just below Monarch Spring. Here, the canyon bends sharply to the right and narrows. Hiking below the spring would be difficult due to dense vegetation and loose, rocky side slopes. Retrace your route.

10
KEANE WONDER SPRING

Highlights: Sulfurous spring, travertine mounds, and historic mine sites.
Type of hike: Out-and-back.
Total distance: 2 miles.
Elevation gain: Minimal.
Best months: Late October–March.
Maps: Trails Illustrated Death Valley National Park Map; USGS Chloride City quad.
Parking and trailhead facilities: There is a parking area at the end of the gravel road.

Finding the trailhead: From Nevada 374 at a point 19.3 miles southwest of Beatty, Nevada, turn left (south) on the Daylight Pass Cutoff and drive 4.3 miles to a signed dirt road on your left. Take the gravel road 2.8 miles to Keane Wonder Mine parking area.

From Furnace Creek, go north on California 190 for 11.3 miles from the visitor center. Turn right (east) on the Daylight Pass Cutoff, and drive 5.7 miles to the Keane Wonder gravel road on your right. Drive 2.8 miles to Keane Wonder Mine parking area. The trail to the spring begins at the northeastern corner of the parking area and heads north.

Keane Wonder Spring

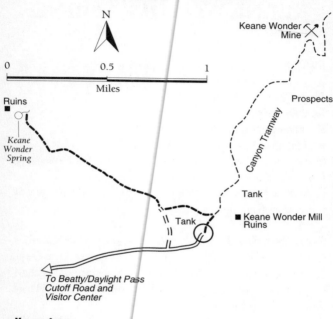

Key points:
0.0 The trail heads north above the pair of settling tanks.
0.3 The trail crosses a wash.
0.6 The trail merges with a trail from the lower hillside; continue on the trail to the spring and mine site.
0.8 The first spring-fed stream crosses the trail. An aqueduct ditch parallels trail.
1.0 Reach the mine chute, cabin, and another sulphur seep.

The hike: The Keane Wonder Mine complex was at its height during the gold boom of 1906 to 1912. Optimistic prospectors and investors have resuscitated it several times since then. The most recent renaissance was in 1935–1937, when cyanide leaching of the mine tailings took place on the site. The tanks used for that operation stand below the parking area.

The mine trail goes directly up the hillside, while the route to Keane Wonder Spring goes left (west). The trail begins after you drop into the debris-strewn wash just north of the parking area. Emerging from the wash above the pair of settling tanks nestled together, you pick up the well-traveled trail. A broken pipeline lies 50 yards below on the hillside along your pathway to the springs.

The trail travels by numerous mine openings and scenic travertine rock outcroppings. At 0.6 mile, the trail merges with another path coming up from lower on the hillside; you can return to the parking area via the lower trail on the hike back. More mine openings and a stone foundation are nearby. The trail is meticulously bordered with rocks for most of the way.

Continuing northward, your nose will detect the scent of sulfur, even on a windy day. At 0.8 mile, the trickling stream from the spring crosses the road. Above the trail, take a side trip to the spring. A salt grass marsh flourishes in the salt-encrusted soil 30 yards above the trail. A National Park Service sign warns of gas hazards in the mineshaft immediately above the spring. The area has many mine shafts, some flooded, all dangerous.

This mining wasteland is also full of wildlife. Heavy use by bighorn sheep is evident from the droppings on the damp spring banks. Birds and crickets create a symphony of sound in the desert stillness.

Continuing northward, the trail follows a crude aqueduct and curves around, now totally out of sight of the parking area and the industrial sprawl located there. Ubiquitous mine sites and another sulfurous spring bracket the trail. At 1 mile—your destination—you'll find a mine chute and a miner's cabin. Rusty cans, pipe pieces, and the usual nondescript rusty artifacts litter the ground. In the dry desert air, the cabin is so well preserved it appears the miner left recently. A large rock outcropping lies atop a hill across the shallow gully to the west. Notice the stone walls built under the natural overhang. Did wind, or heat, or both force the miner to take refuge in such a primitive rock shelter?

Return the way you came, continuing on the wide rock-lined trail at the junction you passed on the way in. In sight of the parking area, the trail dissipates in the mine debris in the gully near the largest of the remaining tanks. From there, you have to pick your way back to your vehicle.

The amazing thing about the Keane Wonder Spring hike is its plethora of mine sites. Keane Wonder Mine was heralded to be the richest gold strike in Death Valley, attracting a multitude of hopeful miners. At its peak nearly five hundred prospectors were working in the area. Thus, everywhere you look, there's another mine mouth with its tailings dripping down the hillside. Mine tunnels like rabbit holes cut through the ridges and disappear into mountainsides. Mines are sometimes a fatal attraction to the curious. Stay out and stay alive.

Salt Creek Interpretive Trail

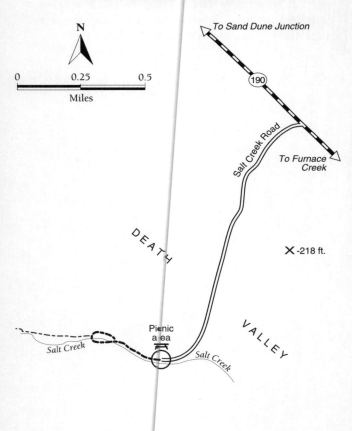

N

0   0.25   0.5
Miles

To Sand Dune Junction

190

To Furnace Creek

Salt Creek Road

DEATH

X -218 ft.

VALLEY

Picnic area

Salt Creek

Salt Creek

11
SALT CREEK
INTERPRETIVE TRAIL

Highlights: Unique vegetation and wildlife such as pupfish, pickleweed, and salt grass.
Type of hike: Loop.
Total distance: 0.5 mile.
Elevation gain: Minimal.
Best months: February–April.
Maps: Trails Illustrated Death Valley National Park Map; USGS Beatty Junction quad.
Parking and trailhead facilities: The parking area and signed interpretive trail are at the end of the road.

Finding the trailhead: From California 190, at a point 2.4 miles northwest of Beatty Junction and 4 miles south of Sand Dune Junction, turn southwest on the Salt Creek Road and drive 1.2 miles to the Salt Creek Interpretive Trail. From the park visitor center in Furnace Creek, drive north on CA 190 for 13.8 miles and turn left (southwest) on the signed road to the Salt Creek Interpretive Trail.

Key points:
0.0 The boardwalk begins west of the parking area.
0.1 Go straight to the first bridge for proper number sequence.

0.2 The use trail at the end of the loop leads up Salt Creek toward Devils Cornfield; continue on the boardwalk to return to the parking area.

The hike: Salt Creek Interpretive Trail is a fully accessible, lollipop-shaped boardwalk hike, with trailside signs providing interpretive information. The extended hike continues 4.5 miles up Salt Creek to the Devils Cornfield on CA 190. There is a beach-like quality to the short hike, not only due to the boardwalk designed to protect this delicate habitat, but also due to the aroma of salt water, and the salt grass and pickleweed growing in dense clumps on the sandy stream banks.

The Salt Creek pupfish, endemic to Death Valley, are the stars of this hike. It's hard to believe these tiny relicts of the Ice Age can continue living in the hottest, driest place in the United States. In the spring, hundreds of pupfish swim in the riffles and pools of the creek. The fish are only visible February through May, with peak activity during March and early April. In other seasons they are either dormant (winter), or the stream is reduced to isolated pools (summer and fall).

The boardwalk runs alongside the creek and then crosses it in several spots—the first bridge is at 0.1 mile—so it provides an excellent vantage point to watch the pupfish in the clear shallow water or the deep pools. Pupfish are fast, small (not much longer than an inch), and enjoy zipping up and down the shallow riffles to bunch up in schools in the deeper terminal pools. As prehistoric Lake Manly dried up and grew saltier, these little fish were able to adapt to the new salty environment. Slimy green and brown algae, caddis flies, beetles, and water boatmen flourish here too, providing an adequate diet for the pupfish.

The walk out along Salt Creek is a startling change from the usual Death Valley desert floor hike. The sound of the merry running water in the winter and spring, with the flourishing growth of salt grasses, suggests a stroll on the beach. All that are missing are the seagulls. With the interpretive signs along the trail, you can enjoy the fish and birds as well as learn about the dynamic changes of the desert habitat and the ability of some species to adapt to its harsh conditions.

Option: To leave the developed boardwalk trail, take the use trail from the far (west) end of the loop at 0.2 mile. The path heads north along the east side of Salt Creek. You can amble along the path, out and back, for as far as you want. Along the way you'll see more pupfish and a variety of birds. This is a good place to spot a great blue heron.

Grotto Canyon
Mosaic Canyon

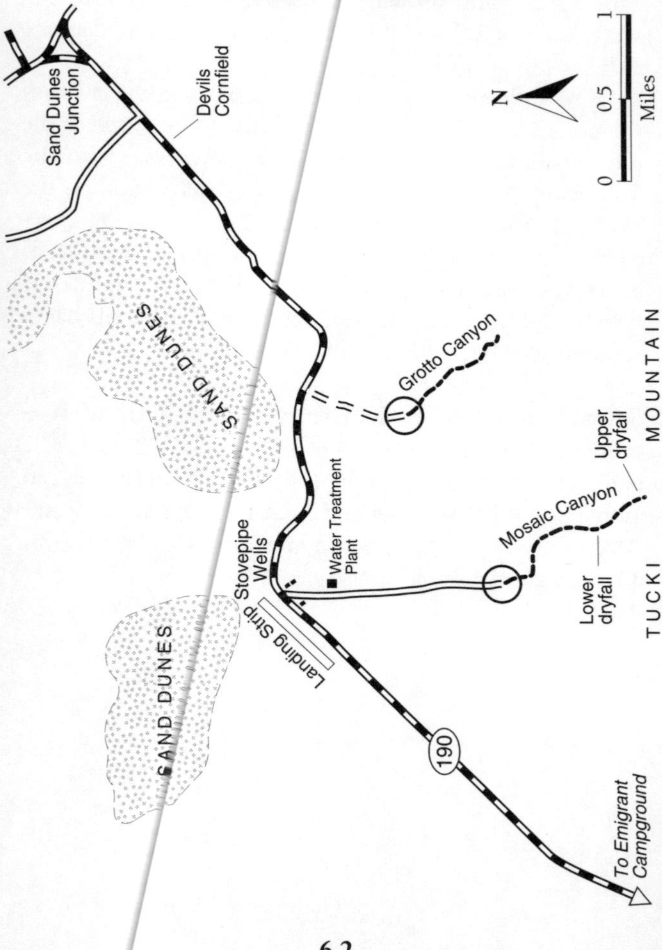

N

0   0.5   1
Miles

Sand Dunes Junction

Devils Cornfield

SAND DUNES

Grotto Canyon

Water Treatment Plant

Stovepipe Wells

Upper dryfall

Mosaic Canyon

Lower dryfall

TUCKI   MOUNTAIN

SAND DUNES

Landing Strip

190

To Emigrant Campground

12
GROTTO CANYON

Highlights: Water-carved grottos.
Type of hike: Out-and-back.
Total distance: 4 miles.
Elevation gain: 540 feet.
Best months: October–April.
Maps: Trails Illustrated Death Valley National Park Map; USGS Grotto Canyon quad.
Parking and trailhead facilities: There is a parking area at the end of the dirt road.

Finding the trailhead: The Grotto Canyon access road heads south from California 190, 2.4 miles east of Stovepipe Wells Village and 3.9 miles west of Sand Dunes Junction. The road is signed for Grotto Canyon and four-wheel-drive vehicles. The road ends for most vehicles after 1.1 miles above the wash, which is soft gravel. The road/trail continues up the wash to the canyon.

Key points:
0.0 Follow the gravel jeep road up the wash.
0.9 The canyon narrows.
1.8 Reach the first dryfall.
2.0 Arrive at the second dryfall.

The hike: With careful driving, a passenger vehicle can negotiate the road to the wash of the Grotto Canyon hike. For the mile to the canyon entrance, the wash's soft gravel requires high clearance and four-wheel drive. No signs or markers punctuate the end of the road, but severe washouts end vehicle access just before the first dryfall. Conditions in this canyon change with each flood. At times the gravel is deep and the dryfalls easy to scale, but often floods have scoured away the gravel, making exploration more of a challenge.

Like the other Tucki Mountain canyons, Grotto Canyon is very broad—up to 200 yards wide in many areas. Deeply eroded canyon walls stand like medieval castle ramparts, with short serpentine pathways in their lower reaches. The narrows at 1.8 miles bring welcome shade after the journey up the graveled canyon bottom. A pair of ravens nesting in the aerie alcove above the grotto may provide suitable visual and sound effects for the hiker approaching this almost cave-like section of the canyon. About 0.1 mile back down the canyon, a trail marked with cairns on the eastern side leads you around this barrier to the canyon above. Another dryfall at 2.0 miles will block your travels.

Even with its proximity to Stovepipe Wells, Grotto Canyon is not heavily visited. The adventuresome hiker can enjoy desert exploration and solitude without a lengthy drive. The intense silence above Mesquite Flat rings in your ears between cries of the ravens.

Hiking back to the road, the dunes stretch out below, framed by the Cottonwood and Grapevine Mountains. Grotto Canyon is a desert wonder of a smaller dimension.

13
MOSAIC CANYON

see map page 62

Highlights: Patterned walls of multicolored rock, and water-sculpted formations.
Type of hike: Out-and-back.
Total distance: 2.8 miles to the lower dryfall.
Elevation gain: 530 feet to the lower dryfall.
Best months: October–April.
Maps: Trails Illustrated Death Valley National Park Map; USGS Stovepipe Wells quad.
Parking and trailhead facilities: There is a parking area at the end of a rough dirt road.

Finding the trailhead: Go 0.1 mile southwest of Stovepipe Wells Village on California 190, then head south on the rough but passable Mosaic Canyon Road (signed). After 2.1 miles the road ends at the Mosaic Canyon parking area. The trail takes off immediately (south).

Key points:
- 0.0 The trail follows the wash from the parking area behind the information sign.
- 0.2 Enter the canyon.
- 1.4 A 40-foot dryfall blocks the canyon; 50 yards back, cairns and arrows mark the side trail for the longer option.

The hike: The fault in Tucki Mountain that produced Mosaic Canyon consists of mosaic breccia and smooth Noonday formation dolomite, formed in a seabed 750 to 900 million years ago. After being pressurized and baked at more than 1,000 degrees, then eroded, the resulting rock has startling contrasts of both texture and color.

Mosaic Canyon drains more than 4 square miles of the Tucki Range, so avoid it, like all canyons, in flashflood conditions. Rushing water, carrying its load of scouring boulders, has created smooth marbleized waterways out of the otherwise lumpy breccia. Silky surfaces on the canyon floor gradually change to rugged lumps higher up its walls, reflecting the varying depths of floodwaters.

Like other canyons in Tucki Mountain, Mosaic Canyon is alternatively wide and narrow. The wider spots are more numerous and broad enough almost to qualify as inner valleys. Often hikers arrive at these open areas and turn back, figuring the canyon excitement has ended. With plenty of water and a broad-brimmed hat, you can continue exploring the depths of Mosaic Canyon. If it's a hot day, be aware this is not a deep shady canyon like those in the Grapevine and Funeral Mountains. This canyon offers little protection from the sun.

The first 0.2 mile of canyon features the polished marble surfaces that have made Mosaic Canyon a favorite destination of Death Valley visitors. After that, the canyon opens to a wide colorful amphitheater, swinging eastward to a broad valley with a 40-foot butte standing in the center. Use trails go in all directions, converging at the end of the valley where the canyon narrows again. To the right of the butte, a deep wash will eventually become a new branch of Mosaic Canyon.

At 1 mile, a small pile of boulders blocks a narrow spot. A well-traveled path to the left (east) provides an easy detour. After another wide spot, the canyon narrows again, where an abrupt 40-foot dryfall blocks your passage at 1.4 miles. The hike back down the canyon provides new views of Death Valley and the Cottonwood Mountains in the distance. Sliding down the short water chutes on the return to the trailhead increases the marbleized beauty of these breccia formations; generations of hikers have added to water's erosive force in creating these smooth rocks.

You can sometimes see bighorn sheep above Mosaic Canyon, so keep a watchful eye out for these reclusive desert denizens.

Option: It is possible to get around the dryfall on a well-traveled, marked trail. Drop 50 yards back from the dryfall to the trail on the sloping canyon wall to the south. This trail takes you to the upper region of Mosaic Canyon, where another 0.5 mile and 320 feet of elevation gain through marbleized chutes and narrows awaits you. A steep marble funnel, 50 feet high, halts the hike at about 2 miles. It's a striking spot, with eroding, fragmented Tucki Mountain rising above the silky smooth waterslide.

14
LOWER MARBLE CANYON

Highlights: Deep canyon narrows; colorful rock bands; petroglyphs.
Type of hike: Out-and-back.
Total distance: 4.6 miles from the road closure 2.6 miles up Marble Canyon Road; if you park at the signed Cottonwood-Marble junction, add 5.2 miles to the round-trip hiking distance.
Elevation gain: 1,000 feet.
Best months: October–May.
Maps: Trails Illustrated Death Valley National Park Map; USGS Cottonwood Creek quad.
Parking and trailhead facilities: There is space for parking at either the road junction or at the end of the rough Marble Canyon dirt road, at the barrier and sign.

Finding the trailhead: From Stovepipe Wells Village on California 190, head west on the Cottonwood Creek Road. The Cottonwood Creek Road begins by bearing left at the entrance to the Stovepipe Wells Campground. The two-wheel-drive portion of this slow, rocky road ends after 8.4 miles, when the road drops steeply into Cottonwood Wash and turns left (south) up the canyon. High-clearance four-wheel drive is advised beyond this point due to soft gravel and high centers. The junction of the

Lower Marble Canyon

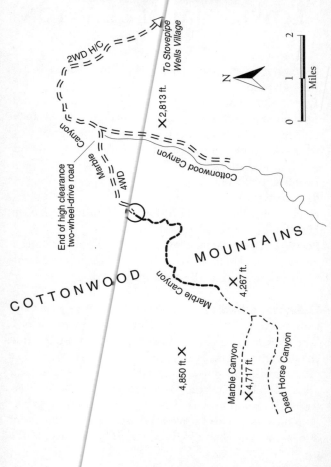

To Stovepipe Wells Village

2WD H/C

×2,813 ft.

N

Miles

0 1 2

End of high clearance
two-wheel-drive road

Cottonwood Canyon

Marble Canyon

4WD

COTTONWOOD

MOUNTAINS

Marble Canyon

4,850 ft. ×

×
4,267 ft.

Marble Canyon
×4,717 ft.

Dead Horse Canyon

Cottonwood and Marble Canyon Roads is 10.7 miles from the Stovepipe Wells Campground. Cottonwood Canyon is to the left (south). The Marble Canyon Road continues to the right (southwest) for another 2.6 miles to the signed vehicle closure at the canyon narrows. Park at the junction of Marble and Cottonwood Canyons if you have any doubts about whether your vehicle can negotiate these final, very rough 2.6 miles.

Key points:
0.0 The trailhead is at the signed vehicle closure on Marble Canyon Road.
0.3 The canyon to the right leads to a 15-foot dry falls; stay left.
1.1 A huge boulder blocks the canyon; climb up stepping stones to the right.
1.4 Overhangs create a cave-like effect in the canyon.
2.3 Reach a major junction; the left (west) branch is a narrow, dark-walled canyon.

Optional extended hike:
3.5 The canyon narrows; a semicircular alcove is on the right.
4.0 A boulder blocks the narrow canyon; climb a staircase of rocks on the left.
4.8 Deadhorse Canyon enters from the south.

The hike: The adjacent Cottonwood and Marble Canyons are as different from each other as night and day. Cottonwood is wide and open, whereas Marble is a wonderland of intimate narrows and dark alcoves. As such, the recommended trip described below is an out-and-back exploration of scenic lower Marble Canyon.

Marble Canyon is susceptible to flash flooding, with a corresponding danger of being caught in one of its steep chutes with no escape. Do not attempt to hike the canyon if wet weather appears imminent.

The hike might start out of vehicular necessity at the Cottonwood Canyon and Marble Canyon road junction, but the real adventure begins 2.6 miles up the canyon at the gap and road closure. On the way, up at mile 2.3, you can see petroglyphs at the mouth of the canyon. Sadly, vandals have senselessly defaced some of these irreplaceable cultural links to the past. You can view other, more pristine petroglyphs farther up Marble Canyon.

At the trailhead, the canyon is only about 6 feet wide. A sign marks the wilderness boundary and closure to vehicles. At 0.3 mile, a canyon enters from the right (north) that leads quickly to a 15-foot dry fall. Continue left (west) up the Mormon tea and creosote-lined bottom next to great stair-step beds of tilted gray and red rock.

At 1.1 miles, bypass the huge boulder blocking the canyon by climbing up stepping stones on the right. At 1.3 miles, the canyon narrows to sheer, gray cliffs where graffiti mars still more petroglyphs. Here, every turn in the twisting canyon brings new variety, with arches being formed from smooth, gently eroded gray cliffs. Overhangs create an almost cave-like effect.

At 1.6 miles the valley opens dramatically, only to narrow again at 1.9 miles. Once more, at 2.3 miles, the valley widens with brilliant displays of reds, tans, and grays on both sides. A major canyon enters from the right (north). The left (west) fork is a dark-walled narrows that soon gives way to a long, open stretch. This junction is the turnaround point for the short hike.

Option: Depending on your time and energy, you can extend this canyon day hike another 2.5 miles to the mouth of Deadhorse Canyon. After the long, open stretch referred to above, the canyon closes in again at 3.5 miles, marked by a distinctive semicircular alcove on the left. Soon, white and gray bands of marble resembling zebra stripes border a wonderland of grottos in the narrow canyon. A second large boulder blocks the wash at 4 miles, which can be easily bypassed by climbing a "staircase" rock on the left. A small side canyon, overlooked by buttes and pinnacles, enters on the right at 4.2 miles.

Deadhorse Canyon joins Marble Canyon from the south (left) at 4.8 miles. The wide Deadhorse valley looks deceptively like the main drainage, but Marble Canyon cuts sharply to the right (west). Many years ago someone etched "Gold Belt Spring 4 miles" into the desert varnish of a large rock with an arrow pointing up Marble Canyon. Another 0.2 mile above the junction, a massive white cliff oversees the left side of Marble Canyon as it climbs steeply toward Goldbelt Spring.

As you return down the canyon to the trailhead, you'll appreciate having had the sun at your back for both the morning and afternoon descent. This trip is well worth a full day of canyon exploration.

15
WILDROSE TRAIL

Highlights: Historic charcoal kilns, a rugged canyon, and scenic views of Death Valley.

Type of hike: Out-and-back.

Total distance: 3.6 miles.

Elevation gain: 850 feet to saddle; 2,274 feet to the summit of Wildrose Peak.

Best months: September–mid-November; March-June (depending on snow levels).

Maps: Trails Illustrated Death Valley National Park Map; USGS Telescope Peak quad, plus the Wildrose Peak quad for those climbing the peak.

Parking and trailhead facilities: There is a signed trailhead at the parking area.

Finding the trailhead: From California 190 at Emigrant Junction, drive south on the Emigrant Canyon Road for 20.9 miles to Wildrose Junction; continue east on the Mahogany Flat Road (paved for 4.5 miles) and drive 7.1 miles to the Wildrose Charcoal Kilns parking area. In winter this road may be impassable; check with park authorities for weather and road conditions. The signed trail to Wildrose Peak begins at the west end of the kilns.

Wildrose Trail

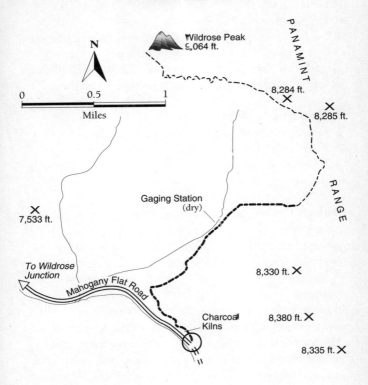

N

0   0.5   1
Miles

Wildrose Peak
9,064 ft.

PANAMINT

8,284 ft.
X

X
8,285 ft.

RANGE

Gaging Station
(dry)

X
7,533 ft.

To Wildrose
Junction

Mahogany Flat Road

8,330 ft. X

Charcoal
Kilns

8,380 ft. X

8,335 ft. X

Key points:
0.0 Trailhead.
0.9 Reach the head of Wildrose Canyon.
1.2 Pass the defunct water gaging station; trail bends and steepens.
1.8 Climb the saddle; views of Death Valley and Badwater open to the east. The trail turns north.

Optional climb to Wildrose Peak:
2.9 Reach a second saddle with more panoramas.
4.1 Arrive on the south peak, the false summit.
4.2 On the north peak, the genuine summit, you will find a register in an ammo box.

The hike: The Wildrose Trail is one of only two constructed trails in the park. It travels through classic pinyon pine–juniper forest to a high saddle, then zigzags to the broad, open summit of this central peak in the Panamint Range.

In spite of the impressive elevation gain to the peak, Wildrose Trail begins modestly. From the kilns at the trailhead, the trail charges 50 yards uphill to the north-west, gaining 60 feet, but then follows the contour of the hillside for the next mile. This section is a gentle warm-up for those climbing the peak. Along the route, rock outcroppings extend to the west, hovering over Wildrose Canyon below. This is classic mountain lion country.

Climbing only slightly, the trail joins an old logging trail coming up from the canyon. Numerous pine stumps are a reminder of the logging done here more than a century ago to supply the charcoal kilns during their brief use in the 1870s.

At the head of the canyon at 0.9 mile, the trail begins its climb. At 1.2 miles, the remains of a USGS water gaging station stand on the left (northwest) side of the trail. There is no longer any groundwater to measure. From the gaging station, the trail bends north and steepens sharply, gaining more than 600 feet in less than a mile. Rising to the first saddle at 1.8 miles, you have a magnificent view through the evergreens of Death Valley below. Unless climbing the peak, this is a good turn-around point.

Option: Wildrose Peak provides panoramic views of Death Valley and the surrounding mountain ranges. This broad, open summit in the central Panamint Range is reached via an 8.4-mile round-trip hike, with a vertical gain of 2,274 feet. Telescope Peak and Wildrose Peak are served by maintained trails and are the only hikes recommended during summer because of extreme heat at lower elevations. Parts of the Wildrose Trail may be icy and snow covered from November through April.

The trail climbs around three small rises before emerging on a ridge above the saddle below the peak. Here, at 3.1 miles and 8,230 feet, you can pause and view the 90-mile length of Death Valley. From the saddle, a mile of switchbacks leads to the summit. The trail snakes north, then south, then north, and so on, up the 800-foot climb. The changing direction enables you to enjoy a variety of vistas as you ascend the mountain, particularly as you near the windswept summit, which is clear of major vegetation. The meadow-like mountaintop is nearly always windy; appropriate clothing is a requirement, as are binoculars to enjoy the sweeping 360-degree view. Summer hikers will appreciate bug dope to combat flies and gnats.

A small rock wall on the peak was designed to give some protection from the wind. Or you can drop just a couple of feet down on the leeward side of the mountain to enjoy your stay and write a note for the peak registry. From Wildrose, you can see the vast area of mining activity in the north end of the Panamint Range. Just to the northeast, in the canyon below, there is a massive mining camp. Farther along Emigrant Canyon Road, mining roads crisscross the mountainsides. Rogers (with the microwave station) and Telescope Peaks loom above to the south. To the west is the mighty wall of the Sierras. To the east, across the valley, rise the Funeral and Black Mountains.

The hike back down the mountain allows you to relax and focus on a new view of the scenery. Death Valley Canyon, extending eastward below the high saddle, is just one of the dramatic sights you may notice on the downward trip. Although this is a heavily used trail, its bending pathway preserves a feeling of solitude for the hiker.

16
NEMO CANYON

Highlights: A gentle downhill traverse, colorful rock formations, several short, narrow side canyons.
Type of hike: Shuttle.
Total distance: 3.6 miles.
Elevation loss: 1,383 feet.
Best months: October–May.
Maps: Trails Illustrated Death Valley National Park Map; USGS Emigrant Pass quad.
Parking and trailhead facilities: Park at the end of an unsigned gravel road at a paved T intersection.

Finding the trailhead: From Wildrose Junction (0.2 mile west of the Wildrose Campground and ranger station), drive 2.2 miles north on the paved Emigrant Canyon Road. Turn left (northwest) onto an unsigned gravel road that takes off from the paved road as it veers right (northeast). Drive 0.7 mile to the end of the road at a paved T next to a gravel pit. A USGS benchmark is adjacent to this spot, which is the trailhead and jumping-off point for the hike. The end point is the broad mouth of Nemo Canyon on the Wildrose Canyon Road, which is located down the canyon 3 miles southwest of Wildrose Junction and one mile southwest of the picnic area.

Nemo Canyon

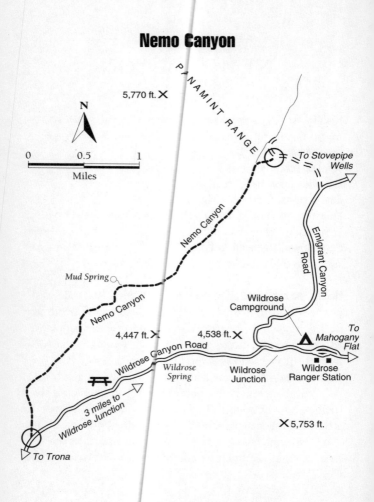

5,770 ft. ✕

PANAMINT RANGE

N

0   0.5   1
Miles

To Stovepipe Wells

Nemo Canyon

Mud Spring ○

Nemo Canyon

Wildrose Campground

4,447 ft. ✕   4,538 ft. ✕

Emigrant Canyon Road

To Mahogany Flat

Wildrose Canyon Road

Wildrose Spring

Wildrose Junction

Wildrose Ranger Station

3 miles to Wildrose Junction

✕ 5,753 ft.

To Trona

Key points:
0.0 The trailhead is in Nemo Canyon wash.
1.8 Reach Mud Springs.
3.6 Arrive at Wildrose Canyon Road.

The hike: This down-canyon traverse begins in open desert country dotted with creosote brush and Mormon tea. Nemo Canyon drops moderately to the southwest. To avoid walking toward the sun and into a stiff afternoon wind, make this a morning excursion if at all possible.

The canyon is wide open with low-lying hills and ridges—a pleasing contrast to nearby mountain climbs. Soon, a few scattered yucca begin to appear. At first the wash is braided and graveled but it becomes better defined, with a sandy bottom, after about one mile. At 1.5 miles the valley narrows a bit. After another 0.2 mile, red rhyolite bluffs rise on the left (south) side. Around the corner the valley opens in a semicircle, with several side canyons entering from the right (north). The white saline seep of Mud Spring is also to the right (north) at 1.8 miles.

At 2 miles, 100-foot-high cliffs rise on the left (south) as the canyon narrows slightly. After another 0.2 mile the wash parallels brightly colored badlands—red, white, black, gray, pink, and tan—with steep bluffs rising several hundred feet on the left. At 2.4 miles a huge valley enters from the right (north). At 3.0 miles, the canyon is marked by brown, deeply eroded conglomerate cliffs and spires. Large granite boulders appear, resting precariously atop spires of brown conglomerate. At times loose gravel impedes walking, but the steady downhill grade helps.

At 3.5 miles the canyon opens to the wide Wildrose Valley. In just another 0.1 mile, Nemo Canyon meets the rough Wildrose Canyon Road, thereby completing this point-to-point downhill traverse.

17
LOWER DARWIN FALLS

Highlights: Bird watching along a year-round desert stream, with high waterfalls in a densely vegetated canyon gorge.
Type of hike: Out-and-back
Total distance: 1.6 miles.
Elevation gain: Minimal.
Best months: October–June.
Maps: Trails Illustrated Death Valley National Park Map; USGS Darwin quad.
Parking and trailhead facilities: There is a signed trailhead parking area at the end of the rough dirt road.

Finding the trailhead: From Panamint Springs, 29.6 miles southwest of Stovepipe Wells on California 190, drive west for 1.1 miles to the signed Darwin Falls Road on the left. Turn left (southwest) on the dirt road, and drive 2.6 miles to the signed side road on the right (south) for Darwin Falls. You will notice a pipeline running along the road. The road is rough but passable for a standard passenger vehicle. Continue another 0.2 mile, dropping into the Darwin Falls streambed/wash, to the signed trailhead parking area.

Key points:
0.0 The trail follows the stream up the narrow valley floor.

Lower Darwin Falls

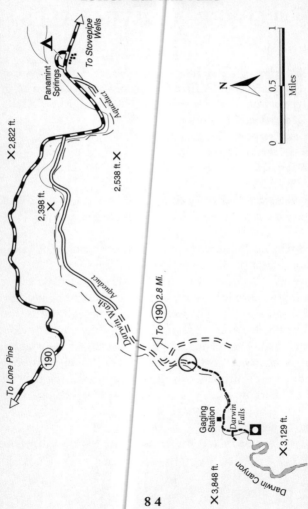

To Stovepipe Wells

Panamint Springs

Aqueduct

X 2,822 ft.

2,398 ft. X

2,538 ft. X

Darwin Wash Aqueduct

To Lone Pine

190

To 190 2.8 Mi.

Gaging Station

Darwin Falls

X 3,129 ft.

Darwin Canyon

X 3,848 ft.

N

Miles

1

0.5

0

0.4 Pass a vehicle barricade at the entrance to the canyon.
0.7 A USGS stream gaging station is on the right bank.
0.8 Reach the lower falls.

Optional hike:
0.8 Drop back downstream for 50 yards to pick up the
     trail to the middle valley and overlook.
0.9 Reach the middle valley; thread your way through
     willows to the high basin and pools below the falls
     at 1 mile. Return to the same trail to ascend to
     the overlook.

The hike: Nestled at the western edge of the expansion
area of Death Valley National Park, Darwin Falls was
formerly a BLM Area of Critical Environmental Con-
cern (ACEC). During its years of jurisdiction, the BLM
took firm measures to protect the area against vehicular
intrusion. Welded pipe barricades are still in place, along
with stern warnings against such misuse. The BLM's
8,600-acre Darwin Falls Wilderness Area is immediately
west of the park adjacent to the canyon.

Darwin Stream is the only permanent water in this
area of the park. Flowing from the China Garden Spring,
Darwin supplies the Panamint Springs Resort with water via a pipeline visible on both the drive and the hike to
the falls. This year-round water source sustains dense
willow and cottonwood thickets in the valley and canyon, as well as a thriving bird population. Cliff swallows
and red-tailed hawks soar overhead, and are among the

more than 80 bird species that have been seen here. Brazen chuckwallas stare at intruders from their rocky lairs.

This hike is a radical change from the usual Death Valley outing. Right from the parking area, a streak of greenery and a glistening brook lead up the gently sloping valley floor. Hopping from one side of the stream to the other begins here, and continues throughout the hike. Steady footwork will prevent getting soaked, but you should exercise care on the smooth slippery boulders farther up the canyon. The Darwin Mountains, composed of black rhyolite, tower above the bright green grass, the willow saplings, the horsetails, and cattails.

At the notch of the canyon's mouth, another welded barricade remains, as does a BLM sign reminding visitors of Darwin Falls' value to vegetation and to wildlife. Because this is a public water supply, bathing and wading are prohibited. The high, dry trail is above the stream on the south side of the canyon.

There are many bends in the narrow canyon. With the steep canyon walls, as well as the willow and cottonwood thickets, this is a shady hike and an excellent outing for a hot, sunny day! A USGS gaging station on the north side of the stream at 0.7 mile, with its aluminum phone booth architecture, looks decidedly out of place in this Garden of Eden.

At 0.8 mile, you reach the falls, after hearing them in the distance. Double falls cascade over a 25-foot dropoff, surrounded by large old cottonwoods. Sword ferns, watercress, and cattails flourish in the pool below. This is the turnaround point for the shorter hike.

Emerging from Darwin Canyon is an Alice-in-Wonderland experience. After being surrounded by humidity and greenery, the beige world of the desert looks one-dimensional. The valley below the canyon is a striking transition zone, with the soft greenery of the stream ecosystem juxtaposed against the jagged dark rhyolite cliffs of the mountains to the south. The hike to Darwin Falls is a carnival of sensory perceptions. The smells, sounds, feel, and sights of this watery world make this an exceptional experience.

Option: To explore farther, retreat 50 yards downstream from the falls and pick up the use trail on the south wall. The best option (there are several use trails) takes off on a solid outcropping of greenish granite and traverses the canyon wall to the valley above the fall. Climb the finely grained granite with caution. It doesn't crumble, but it can be very slippery. From the trail, thread your way through the dense willows and cottonwoods to the upper end of the valley adjacent to a very loose talus slope. Here, at 0.9 mile, the three-tiered upper falls plummet 140 feet from the cliff above. This is not a heavily visited spot. In the narrow canyon your only company will likely be the cliff swallows swooping overhead.

Titus Canyon Narrows and Fall Canyon

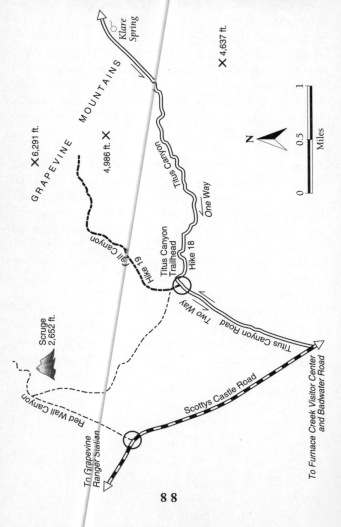

18
TITUS CANYON NARROWS

Highlights: Majestic cliffs, arched caverns, deep narrow canyon.
Type of hike: Out-and-back.
Total distance: 4.2 miles.
Elevation gain: 250 feet.
Best months: October–April.
Maps: Trails Illustrated Death Valley National Park Map; USGS Fall Canyon quad.
Parking and trailhead facilities: The parking area is alongside the dirt road.

Finding the trailhead: The two-way road to the mouth of Titus Canyon is 11.9 miles north of the junction of Scottys Castle Road (California 374) and CA 190, and 17.9 miles south of the Grapevine Ranger Station on the Scottys Castle Road. Take the signed dirt road east for 2.7 miles up the alluvial fan to the Titus Canyon mouth, where there is a parking area. The Titus Canyon Road is one-way from the east, beginning at the canyon mouth. Embark on this hike early in the morning to reduce the chance of meeting vehicles; the 26-mile length of the Titus Canyon Road means it is unlikely that vehicles will arrive in the lower section of the canyon before 10 A.M.

Key points:
0.0 Follow the four-wheel-drive road east into Titus Canyon.
2.1 The narrow canyon opens into a broader valley; this is the turnaround for the short hike.

Optional hike:
5.9 Klare Spring is on north side of road; petroglyphs are east of the spring. This is the turnaround for the long hike.

The hike: Titus Canyon is the longest and one of the grandest canyons in Death Valley. Morris Titus was a prospector who disappeared in the canyon in 1906 while searching for help after running out of water. Titus Canyon Road was built in 1926 to serve the town of Leadville, an investor scam that became a ghost town the following year. This 26-mile one-way unpaved road is accessible only by high-clearance vehicles.

Visiting majestic Titus Canyon by vehicle may not be the most satisfactory way to enjoy its scenery. By driving the two-mile two-way portion at the western end of Titus Canyon Road, you can park and hike the dramatic narrows of the canyon. If you get an early start in the morning, you are less likely to encounter vehicles on the road. Driving to the canyon mouth also enables you to omit the alluvial fan hike, so common to canyon hiking in Death Valley.

Titus Canyon is a slot canyon, immediately narrow at its mouth. From the brightness of the desert floor you plunge into the canyon's cool shadows. Cliffs tower hundreds of feet above. Breezes rush down through the funnel of the canyon. The display of cliffs continues without intermission for two miles as you hike up the primitive canyon road. The variety of colors and textures on the canyon walls is immense and ever changing. The limestone layers are twisted and folded; fault lines run at all angles. In addition to the power of the earth's surface to rise and fall and shift, the power of water is visible throughout the slot canyon. The water-smoothed walls indicate the level of flooding. The curves of the canyon's path reveal the erosive power of the swift floods as they roar down the narrow opening with their load of scouring boulders. Flash floods are a real danger in Titus; often the road is closed for days after a storm in the area.

The 2-mile hike through the narrows is overpowering. Like walking down the nave of a European cathedral, hiking up (and later down) Titus is both a soaring experience, but also an immensely humbling one. The Titus Canyon Fault, which created the canyon, slices through the heart of the Grapevine Mountains, laying their innards bare for the geologist and layman both to enjoy. With the road as a walking surface, you can totally devote your attention to the details of this mountain cross-section, a rare occasion in hiking in Death Valley.

Option: For the longer hike, continue up the road another 3.8 miles to Klare Spring. The canyon floor is considerably broader, although quite steep, after you leave the Narrows at 2.1 miles, but the towering peaks of the

Grapevines still provide a spectacular backdrop for the canyon hike. The spring is on the north side of the road at 5.9 miles. Springs are critical habitat for bighorn sheep, which gather nearby in hot summer months. Some marred petroglyphs are above the spring, a reminder that it is both unlawful and boorish to harm such artifacts. Return the way you came, enjoying your downhill trip, thereby completing a long hike of nearly 12 miles.

19
FALL CANYON

see map page 88

Highlights: One of the deepest and most spectacular canyon narrows in the park.
Type of hike: Out-and-back.
Total distance: 6 miles.
Elevation gain: 1,240 feet.
Best months: October–May.
Maps: Trails Illustrated Death Valley National Park Map; USGS Fall Canyon quad.
Parking and trailhead facilities: There is a parking area adjacent to the dirt road with an unsigned trail.

Finding the trailhead: The trailhead is at the mouth of Titus Canyon. The two-way road to the mouth of Titus Canyon takes off 11.9 miles north of the junction of California Highways 374 and 190, and 17.9 miles south of the Grapevine Ranger Station on the Scottys Castle Road. Proceed northeast on the signed Titus Canyon dirt road for 2.7 miles up the alluvial fan to the canyon mouth, where there is a parking area. Follow the distinct but unsigned trail north of the parking area for 0.7 mile to an extensive wash leading to the mouth of Fall Canyon.

Key points:
0.0 The trailhead is at the mouth of Titus Canyon.
0.7 A use trail meets the Fall Canyon wash.
0.8 Reach the mouth of Fall Canyon.
1.3 The canyon narrows.
2.9 Cairns mark a faint scrambling use trail to the right.
3.0 Arrive at the 30-foot dryfall.

Optional hike:
3.1 The canyon narrows.
3.5 The canyon opens up to high peaks and ridges be-
     yond.

The hike: Fall Canyon is a narrow, twisting chasm in the
colorful Grapevine Mountains. Do not attempt this hike
if wet weather appears likely. The canyon is highly susceptible to flash flooding. You could easily be trapped in
one of the narrow stretches of the canyon by a raging
torrent if caught during a mountain storm.

From the parking area at the mouth of Titus Canyon, hike north on an unsigned but easy-to-follow use
trail, climbing gradually across several low ridges and
gullies. At 0.5 mile the trail enters a side wash and then
swings to the right (north) toward Fall Canyon. At 0.7
mile, the use trail tops out above the Fall Canyon wash,
drops into the wide graveled wash, and vanishes after
another 0.1 mile at the canyon mouth. Here, the canyon
floor becomes your path.

At first the canyon is wide, up to 150 feet in places.
At 1.3 miles the walls steepen and close in; dark shadows

fill the bottom, adding to a feeling of intimacy. The canyon quickly opens to a huge amphitheater-alcove, bounded by sheer cliffs on the left (north), bending tightly to the right (southeast). At 1.5 miles, a large rock sits in a wide bottom that opens to colorful bands of red, white, and gray on the cliff faces. Continue left (east) up the main wash. The canyon narrows again at 1.8 miles, its sides pocketed with a myriad of ledges and small alcoves, only to open again with the west rim soaring 1,000 feet overhead.

At 2 miles, a narrow side canyon enters from the left (north) just above a massive boulder that blocks much of the wash. Continue to the right (east) up the main wash next to an isolated rock pinnacle.

Soon the canyon narrows once more, with rock overhangs reaching out above. At 2.2 miles, colorful folded rock dramatizes the powerful forces that continue to shape this rugged landscape. The canyon squeezes to a gap of only 8 feet at 2.6 miles, then widens, and then narrows again at 2.9 miles. A sheer 30-foot-high dryfall is reached at 3 miles. The fall cannot be safely or easily climbed so this is a good turnaround point for an exhilarating 6-mile round-trip exploration of Fall Canyon.

Options: If you want to continue up Fall Canyon, drop back down the wash less than 0.1 mile and look for cairns on the left (south) side (right side of the canyon going up). This bypass around the fall should only be attempted by those with at least moderate rock-climbing skills and experience. Begin by climbing a steep but solid rock pitch to a well-defined use trail that angles above and around the right side of the fall. Exercise caution on the loose gravel directly above the canyon. Immediately above and beyond the fall, the canyon becomes extremely narrow, bounded by sheer cliffs, folded layers of rock, overhangs, and semicircular bends of smooth gray rock. There are a few short rock pitches that can be easily scrambled up.

At 3.2 miles the tight chasm opens to more distant cliffs, but the actual wash remains narrow. At 3.4 miles, a massive boulder blocks most of the wash, with the easiest way around being to the left. Here, the hardest part about turning around is turning around; every steep-walled bend entices further exploration. The gray-walled canyon, polished smooth by the action of water, is left at 3.5 miles, when the valley opens to reddish rhyolite cliffs and peaks. At 4.1 miles dramatic cliffs rise above steep slopes punctuated with jagged columns of dark rhyolite. Anywhere in this stretch provides a good turnaround point. Retrace your route to complete your exploration of this enchanting canyon.

20
THE GRANDSTAND

Highlights: A high rock mound in a gleaming white playa, "moving rocks," isolation, and scenic views.
Type of hike: Out-and-back.
Total distance: 1 mile.
Elevation gain: Minimal.
Best months: October–May.
Maps: Trails Illustrated Death Valley National Park Map; USGS Ubehebe Peak quad.
Parking and trailhead facilities: The parking area is adjacent to the dirt road.

Finding the trailhead: From the junction of the Scottys Castle Road and the Ubehebe Crater Road in the northeastern corner of the park, head northwest on the paved Ubehebe Crater Road. The pavement ends after 5.3 miles at the turnoff to Ubehebe Crater. Continue south on the washboardy, dirt Racetrack Valley Road for 19.7 miles to Teakettle Junction. Take the right-hand turn for Racetrack Valley Road and drive another 5.7 miles to the Grandstand parking area, which is opposite the "grandstand" of gray rocks in the dry lakebed east of the road.

The Grandstand

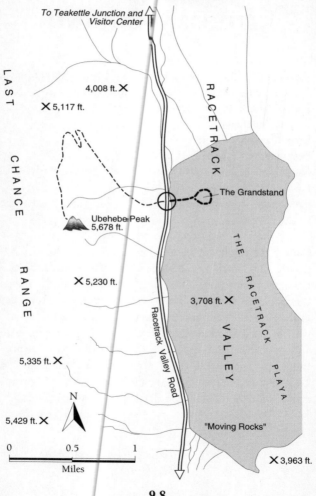

To Teakettle Junction and
Visitor Center

4,008 ft. ✕

✕ 5,117 ft.

L A S T

C H A N C E

R A N G E

✕ 5,230 ft.

5,335 ft. ✕

5,429 ft. ✕

0   0.5   1

Miles

N

R A C E T R A C K

The Grandstand

Ubehebe Peak
5,678 ft.

Racetrack Valley Road

3,708 ft. ✕

T H E

R A C E T R A C K   P L A Y A

V A L L E Y

"Moving Rocks"

✕ 3,963 ft.

Key points:
0.0 Trailhead.
0.5 Reach the Grandstand.

The hike: The Grandstand is about 0.5 mile directly east of the parking area. It consists of a large, 70-foot-high mound of gray rocks rising in stark contrast to the surrounding white flatness of the Racetrack Playa, a dry lakebed. For added perspective, walk around the Grandstand, then scramble up some of the large boulders. The Grandstand can be easily climbed 40 to 50 feet above the playa. Once in awhile rocks fall from the Grandstand to the lakebed, and then they move! Be on the lookout for the tracks of "moving rocks" streaked across the lakebed sediment. The mystery of these mobile rocks is heightened by the fact that no one has ever seen them move. Most likely the rocks are swept by powerful winds when the fine clay surface of the lakebed is made slick by heavy rain. The Grandstand provides a superb perspective of formidable 5,678-foot-high Ubehebe Peak, rising 2,000 feet 1.5 miles to the west.

Options: If time allows, drive south from the Grandstand another 2 miles. Walk to the east across the southern end of the Racetrack Playa. This is where you will find the best view of the mysterious trails of the moving rocks.

A more difficult option is to hike up toward Ubehebe Peak. The trail heads west of the Racetrack Valley Road from the Grandstand parking area. Be sure to carry sufficient water for this high, dry desert climb. The clear trail, originally an old mining path, begins by ascending gradually to the northwest up an alluvial fan clothed with desert trumpet and creosote bush. Within 0.5 mile, the trail begins a long series of steep switchbacks up the east face of the 5,519-foot north peak. This imposing buttress is made even more impressive by broken cliffs of desert varnish. After climbing nearly 1,200 feet in 1.8 miles the trail reaches the north ridge of the peak, which is just beyond an outcropping of limestone where the blue-green copper of malachite rock lines a shallow mine digging. From this point a trail takes off to the right, ending after 0.1 mile at an overlook above an old mine entrance. The summit of Ubehebe Peak can be seen in the distance beyond the north peak, which rises directly above. This is a good turnaround point.

If you wish to continue, take the left-hand trail, which climbs steeply up the ridge through the rocks to 5,160 feet at 2 miles. The trail then wraps around the west side of the mountain, reaching an elevation of 5,440 feet at 2.4 miles. From here on, the trail becomes rougher and more faint, compensated somewhat by stupendous views of the playa to the southeast. The trail then drops for 0.2 mile to the 5,220-foot saddle between the two peaks. Any resemblance to a trail ends at the saddle, which is a good end point for those not wishing to scramble up the steep rocky ridge another 0.4 mile and 460 vertical feet to the top of Ubehebe Peak.

From the saddle, the Saline Valley lies 4,000 feet below to the west. Beyond is the soaring 10,000-foot crest of the Inyo Mountains, with the even higher Sierra Nevada looming farther to the west. The crown of Death Valley—lofty Telescope Peak—can be seen to the southeast, along with the vast wooded plateau of Hunter Mountain. Perhaps most impressive is the eagle's-eye view of the gleaming white Racetrack Playa encircling the tiny dark specks of the Grandstand far below.

Ubehebe Lead Mine

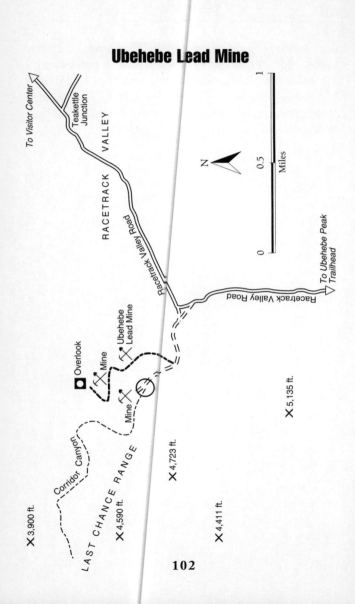

21
UBEHEBE LEAD MINE

Highlights: The remains of an early twentieth-century mine; excellent vistas of cliffs and mountains.
Type of hike: Out-and-back.
Total distance: 1 mile.
Elevation gain: 290 feet.
Best months: October–March.
Maps: Trails Illustrated Death Valley National Park Map; USGS Ubehebe Peak and Teakettle Junction quads.
Parking and trailhead facilities: Park near the end of the dirt road.

Finding the trailhead: From Grapevine Junction, take the Ubehebe Crater Road northwest for 5.5 miles to the end of the pavement and the sign for Racetrack Valley Road. Turn right (southwest) onto Racetrack Valley Road. Four-wheel drive is recommended, but under normal weather conditions is unnecessary. The Racetrack Valley Road is severely washboarded, but contains no other obstacles as far as The Racetrack. Go south on Racetrack Valley Road for 19.6 miles to Teakettle Junction. Bear right (southwest), and continue for 2.2 miles to the right (west) turn to the Ubehebe Lead Mine road (signed). The dirt road leads 0.7 mile to a parking area at the mine site.

Key points:

0.0 Hike back up the road from the miner's shack, on the north side by the low stone wall. The trail leads up the hillside.

0.4 Pass a tram cable tower at the hilltop.

0.5 Arrive at the overlook.

Optional hike:

0.0 Beyond the mine chute, head west down the wash.

0.3 A chute canyon enters from the left (south).

1.0 Reach the dramatic cliffs.

The hike: Ubehebe Mine has a lengthy history, beginning in 1875 when copper ore was found here. The copper mine was not fully developed until early in the twentieth century, but the profitable ore was soon depleted. In 1908, lead mining began at the site and continued until 1928. Ubehebe Mine had another renaissance in the 1940s as a zinc mine. Mining activity came to an end in 1951.

After all this mining it is not surprising to find a plethora of mining artifacts in the valley and in the hills above. A miner's house is still standing; its door and windows ajar, stripped of its plumbing (the range lies outside), it is a well-preserved remnant of its midcentury inhabitants. Remember that it may be unwise to enter deserted buildings due to deer mice and hantavirus.

In the wash above there are other traces of the rude dwellings of miners. Stacked stone walls are still in place. The men worked inside rock walls by day and slept in them at night. Rusty debris and small, level tent sites are

104

scattered about. The usual squeaky bedspring (burned and rusted) lies amid the creosote bushes. This is an appropriate place to pause and contemplate the bustle of activity and spirit of optimism that must have prevailed in this mining valley in its various heydays.

Below the housing area sits the ore chute, with rail tracks still leading from a mine opening. The area looks like it was deserted only a year ago. The sagging old tram cable still hangs from the tower atop the hill to the valley floor at 0.4 mile. Unsecured mine openings dot the hillside. Although the National Park Service has not posted its usual warning signs, do not get close to mines. The tram should also be given a wide berth.

The hike up the trail to the overlook at 0.5 mile gives you a magnificent aerial view of the mine encampment and the rolling hills of the Last Chance Range. Mine openings proliferate like rodent burrows. The rust-colored rock and earth in piles at each opening gives the mining operations an eerie fresh appearance, as if the work here just stopped yesterday, instead of 50 or 100 years ago. Numerous wooden posts mark the mountainside along the trail to designate claims of long-gone prospectors. Crossing carefully beneath the hilltop tram tower, you arrive at trail's end and a view westward of winding Corridor Canyon.

Option: A hike down Corridor Canyon is a nice addition to the Ubehebe Lead Mine hike. From the mine chute, drop generally westward down the wide and graveled wash to the head of Corridor Canyon. At 0.3 mile, a tantalizing narrow stair-step chute of a canyon enters from the left (south), inviting exploration—although large boulders may prevent you from getting very far.

At about 1 mile, impressive cliff walls soar high to the left (south), whereas the right (north) side is marked by folded rock layers altered by fault lines. Below, as the canyon turns left (west), are colorful bands of rock. The cliffs are pockmarked with caverns and other small openings, some of which serve as active dens for animals.

The canyon is unique in that it provides both a closed-in experience, as well as far distant vistas of cliffs, overshadowed by even higher cliff layers beyond, opening to expansive views of adjacent and faraway mountains. The wide wash provides a pleasant day hike extending up to 5 miles one-way.

22
UBEHEBE AND LITTLE HEBE CRATERS

Highlights: Volcanic craters and complex erosion patterns.
Type of hike: Loop.
Total distance: 1.5 miles.
Elevation gain: 320 feet.
Best months: Late October–April.
Maps: Trails Illustrated Death Valley National Park Map; USGS Ubehebe Crater quad.
Parking and trailhead facilities: A signed parking area with an information board is on the paved road.

Finding the trailhead: From the Grapevine Junction of Scottys Castle Road and Ubehebe Crater Road, 45 miles north of Furnace Creek, take Ubehebe Crater Road northwest. Drive 5.7 miles to the parking area for the Ubehebe Crater/Little Hebe Crater trailhead. The parking area is on the eastern side of the one-way loop of paved road at the end of Ubehebe Crater Road.

Key points:
0.0 The trail goes south from the information board at the parking area.
0.1 The trail climbs; bear left at the Y intersection. The trail to the right has eroded on both sides and may be hazardous.

Ubehebe and Little Hebe Craters

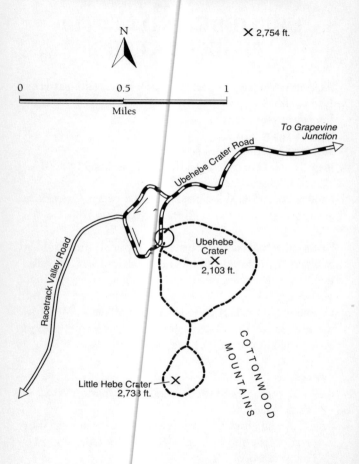

N

✕ 2,754 ft.

0   0.5   1
Miles

To Grapevine
Junction

Ubehebe Crater Road

Racetrack Valley Road

Ubehebe
Crater
✕
2,103 ft.

C O T T O N W O O D
M O U N T A I N S

Little Hebe Crater ✕
2,733 ft.

0.4 Reach a maze of use trails on the small plateau between the craters; a sign directs you south to Little
Hebe Crater. Follow the trail around Little Hebe.
0.7 Back at the intersection, continue to hike around the
large Ubehebe Crater.
1.5 Return to the trailhead or take the optional trail to
the bottom of the crater.

The hike: The volcanic region at the north end of the Cottonwood Mountains, near Scottys Castle, is evidence of
recent cataclysmic events in Death Valley, geologically
speaking. The huge Ubehebe Crater was created around
3,000 years ago when magma heated groundwater and
the pressure from the resulting steam blew the overlying
rock away. This explosion covered 6 square miles of desert
with volcanic debris 150 feet deep. Called a maar vol-
cano by geologists, Ubehebe is a crater without a cone.
The rim has been eroding ever since the explosion, gradually filling the crater with alluvial fans. Quite appropri-
ately, the Shoshone Indians of Death Valley dubbed the
crater "Basket in the Rock."

Little Hebe Crater, directly south, is much younger.
Having exploded about 300 to 500 years ago, it is one of
the newest geologic features of Death Valley. Little Hebe's
rim is neat and well defined, exhibiting little of the erosion that has reduced Ubehebe's edge.

You can learn a lot about the craters by reading the
information on the board and glancing at these mon-
strous holes in the earth. But there is no substitute for
hiking all the way around this monumental display of

volcanic power if you want to really appreciate the dimensions of the Ubehebe complex.

The first quarter of the hike takes you along the rim of the main crater. The size of the hole is overpowering. It is almost a half of a mile from rim to rim. Alluvial fans have formed on the walls as the rains tear down the crater's edges.

In the vicinity of Ubehebe Crater, there are as many as twelve additional craters, all examples of more maar activity. You will see numerous craters in various stages of eroding deterioration. Little Hebe stands out as a jewel of a crater. Neat and trim, this volcanic chasm is only 200 yards across. The younger, fresher rim has barely begun to weather. Volcanic materials are very durable. Clearly visible on the walls of Little Hebe are the layers beneath the earth's surface. Especially noticeable is a thick layer of viscous lava that had oozed from the earth's interior prior to the explosion of Little Hebe.

After the tour around Little Hebe at 0.7 mile, continue your hike around the main crater, which seems even larger after visiting its younger neighbor. A well-defined trail leads around Ubehebe, ending at 1.5 miles. The power of nature to modify the terrain via volcanic action stands in sharp contrast with the more gradual erosive forces that are demonstrated elsewhere in Death Valley. The earth has not finished rearranging its surface here—the forces that created Ubehebe and Little Hebe are merely dormant, not dead.

Option: The 0.3-mile trail into the crater slopes downward from the rim at 1.3 miles. The volcanic cinder trail descends nearly 500 feet to the floor of the crater. After major rainstorms the crater also features a small lake. Most of the time it is dry. The climb back to the parking area requires some exertion due to the skidding quality of the volcanic cinders.

Eureka Dunes

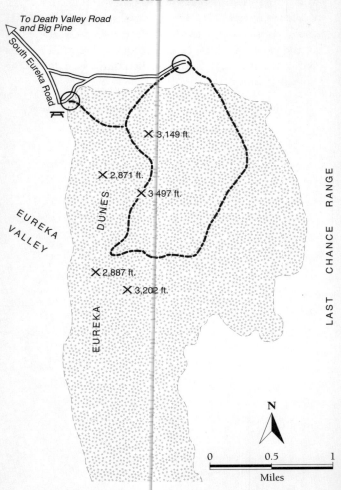

To Death Valley Road
and Big Pine

South Eureka Road

X 3,149 ft.

X 2,871 ft.

X 3,497 ft.

EUREKA
VALLEY

DUNES

X 2,887 ft.

X 3,202 ft.

EUREKA

LAST   CHANCE   RANGE

N

| 0 | 0.5 | 1 |

Miles

23
EUREKA DUNES

Highlights: Remoteness; a scenic backdrop of the colorful Last Chance Mountains, the tallest sand dunes in California and possibly all of North America; endemic plants and animals.

Type of hike: Loop.

Total distance: 3 miles.

Elevation gain: 600 feet.

Best months: October–April.

Maps: Trails Illustrated Death Valley National Park Map; USGS Last Chance Range quad.

Parking and trailhead facilities: You will find a parking area, monument, camping area, picnic tables, and outhouse at the end of the dirt road.

Finding the trailhead: From the south, take Scottys Castle Road to Grapevine Junction and proceed northwest on the Ubehebe Crater Road for 2.8 miles to Big Pine Road, also known as the North Entrance Highway and Death Valley Road. The turnoff is signed "Eureka Dunes 45 miles." Turn north onto the washboard graded gravel Big Pine Road and drive 34 miles to South Eureka Valley Road, the road to the Eureka Dunes. Turn left (south) onto this road and drive 10 miles to the end-of-the-road picnic/parking area near the base of the dunes. From the north, you can reach Eureka Dunes from Big Pine via 28 miles of paved road and 11 miles of graded dirt road. At South Eureka Valley Road, turn right (south) and follow the narrow road for the final 10 miles to the base of the dunes.

Key points:
0.0 Begin from either the picnic tables on the north or the monument in the parking area.
1.5 Begin climbing the east side of the dunes.
2.2 Reach the top of the dunes.
3.0 Arrive at the trailhead.

The hike: For those of us who never completely outgrew our love of sandboxes, this place is paradise. The Eureka Dunes, located within the expanded northern portion of the park, are a fascinating island of sand in a desert sea. From a distance, this 1- by 3-mile mountain of sand seems to hover over the remote Eureka Valley floor. Although not extensive, these dunes are the tallest in California and likely the tallest in North America. From the dry lakebed at their western edge, the Eureka Dunes rise abruptly more than 600 feet. Equally impressive are the sheer faces of the Last Chance Mountains to the immediate east, with their bands of pink, black, and gray limestone.

If the sand here is completely dry, you may hear one of the most unusual sounds in the desert: singing sand. When the sand cascades down the steepest pitch of the highest dune, a rumbling sound comparable to the bass note of a pipe organ emanates from it. No one knows exactly why this happens, but the friction of smooth-textured sand grains sliding against each other probably has something to do with it.

These dunes receive more moisture than others in the park because they are positioned at the western foot of a high mountain range that intercepts passing storms. The isolation of the Eureka Dunes, far from any other dunes, has resulted in endemic plant and animal species. For example, the entire range of five species of beetles and three plants is limited to these lofty mounds.

The three endemic plant species are shining locoweed, Eureka dune grass, and Eureka evening primrose, which are listed as endangered species under the federal Endangered Species Act. Shining locoweed is a hummock-forming plant with root nodules that fix nitrogen from the air, a vital plant nutrient not available in the sand. When wind-blown sand covers the leafy flower shoots of the Eureka evening primrose, a new rosette of leaves forms at the tip. Large, white flowers bloom at night so that moths and other pollinators can avoid daytime heat. Usually, Eureka dune grass is the only plant on the higher slopes of the dunes. Its thick roots hold shifting sand, forming hummocks. Stiff, spiny leaf tips discourage herbivores.

The Eureka Dunes are a small, ecologically unique place requiring special care. Camp and keep vehicles a good distance from the base of the dunes, which is where most of the endemic plants and animals live. If possible, walk where others have in order to concentrate the impact away from pristine areas.

From the monument/parking/camping area, head east cross-country along the base of the dunes toward the color-banded Last Chance Mountains that rise an impressive 4,000 feet above the Eureka Valley floor. Hiking along the base provides a constantly changing perspective of this unusual landscape, as well as a good warm-up for climbing the steep backside of the dunes. A profusion of animal tracks will appear, as will the circular paths of grass tips etched in the sand by the ever-changing wind.

At 0.8 mile, the initial flat stretch becomes laced with gullies strewn with volcanic "bombs" embedded in the sand. At this point, begin curving around the base of the dunes to the right (south). This wonderfully wide-open trek stands in startling contrast to the closed-in feeling one gets when exploring the deep canyons of Death Valley.

At about 1.5 miles, begin climbing westward up any one of the several narrow knife-edge sand ridges that converge at the apex of the dunes. A vertical gain of about 600 feet to the 3,480-foot apex is spread over about 0.7 mile, with most of the climb during the final 0.2 mile. The dry lakebed, expansive Eureka Valley, colorful Last Chance range, and the dunes themselves combine to form a stunning 360-degree panorama. To complete the 3-mile loop, continue back down along narrow ridges and steep scooped-out bowls of sand in a north to northwesterly direction to the trailhead.

Option: Another choice for climbing the dunes, which can be hard work at times in the loose, shifting sand, is a shorter out-and-back route. This more direct approach to the 600-foot climb is a 1.5-mile round-trip hike by way of a series of knife ridges. Because of the long driving distance to the trailhead, the somewhat longer 3-mile loop may be your better choice. In so choosing, you'll gain more intimacy with the dunes and their majestic Last Chance Mountains backdrop.

Afterword

As seasoned hikers accustomed to the high snowy mountains of the Northern Rockies we were excited when the idea of exploring some of the California Desert was presented to us. It would be hard to find two more disparate regions—the California Desert and the Northern Rockies—within the Lower 48. We viewed the opportunity to learn more about such a different ecosystem as a tremendous challenge. And we foresaw many interim challenges along the way, such as the challenge of truly getting to know this splendid country and its hidden treasures beyond the roads. There would be the challenges of climbing rugged peaks, of safely traversing vast expanses of open desert, of navigating across alluvial fans to secluded canyons, of learning enough about the interconnected web of desert geology, flora, and fauna to be able to interpret some of its wonders for others to appreciate. These beckoned to us from blank spots on the park map.

But we each face a far greater challenge—the challenge of wilderness stewardship, which must be shared by all who venture into the wilderness of California's desert parks.

Wilderness stewardship can take many forms, from political advocacy to a leave-no-trace hiking and camping ethic to quietly setting the example of respect for wild country for others to follow. The political concessions that eventually brought about passage of the long-awaited California Desert Protection Act have been made.

Boundaries were gerrymandered, exclusions made, and nonconforming uses grandfathered. Still, the wilderness and park lines that have been drawn in California's desert represent a tremendous step forward in the ongoing battle to save what little remains of our diminishing wilderness heritage.

But drawing lines is only the first step. Now, the great challenge is to take care of what we have. We can each demonstrate this care every time we set out on a hike. It comes down to respect for the untamed but fragile desert, for those wild creatures who have no place else to live, for other visitors, and for those yet unborn who will retrace our hikes into the next century and beyond.

We will be judged not by the mountains we climb but by what we pass onto others in an unimpaired condition. Happy hiking, and may your trails be clear with the wind and sun at your back.

About the Authors

Polly Burke and Bill Cunningham are partners in the long trail of life. Polly, formerly a history teacher in St. Louis, Missouri, now makes her home with Bill in Choteau, Montana. She is pursuing multiple careers in freelance writing, leading group trips in the wilderness, and working with the developmentally disabled. Polly has hiked and backpacked extensively throughout many parts of the country.

Bill is a lifelong "wildernut," as a conservation activist, backpacking outfitter, and field studies teacher for The University of Montana. During the 1970s and 1980s, he was a field representative for The Wilderness Society. He has written several books and dozens of magazine articles about wilderness areas based on extensive on-the-ground knowledge. He is the author of *Wild Montana,* the first in Falcon Publishing's series of guidebooks to wilderness and unprotected roadless areas.

Polly and Bill coauthored Falcon's *Hiking California's Desert Parks* (1996), *Wild Utah* (1998), and *Hiking the Gila Wilderness* (1999). Writing about the vast and varied Death Valley National Park has been especially rewarding because long ago the authors both lived close to the California desert—Bill in Bakersfield and Polly in San Diego. They have enjoyed renewing their ties to California while exploring the state's desert regions. They want others to have as much fun exploring Death Valley as they did.